W9-ATP-218

Praise for *90-Minute College Major Matcher*

"This book is the first of its kind! It actually allows the reader to choose both a major and a career at one reading. This is must reading for anyone who is trying to choose a major and choose a career."

—Dr. John Liptak, Associate Director
Career Assessment and Career Counseling, Radford University

"The *90-Minute College Major Matcher* guides students from indecision to discovering career interest and pathways…and should be issued to every senior in high school as required reading material. In 90 minutes, parents could stop thrashing about wondering how to save money on college expenses, and students would not enter college without a clear idea of a college major. Imagine the time, money, and frustration that could be saved!"

—Linda Schultz, Teacher
MacArthur High School

"Very good information…a resource for career centers...or to give as a gift to graduating high school students...Holland's codes and skills checklist are valuable for students."

—Mary Maddox, Career Counselor
Dallas ISD

90·MINUTE
COLLEGE MAJOR
MATCHER

choose your best major for a great career

LAURENCE SHATKIN, PH.D.

Also in JIST's Help in a Hurry Series

Overnight Career Choice

Same-Day Resume

Next-Day Job Interview

15-Minute Cover Letter

Seven-Step Job Search

90-MINUTE COLLEGE MAJOR MATCHER

© 2007 by JIST Publishing, Inc.

Published by JIST Works, an imprint of JIST Publishing, Inc.
8902 Otis Avenue
Indianapolis, IN 46216-1033

Phone: 1-800-648-JIST   Fax: 1-800-JIST-FAX
E-mail: info@jist.com   Web site: www.jist.com

Visit www.jist.com for information on JIST, free job search information, book excerpts, and ordering information on our many products.

Quantity discounts are available for JIST products. Have future editions of JIST books automatically delivered to you on publication through our convenient standing order program. Please call 1-800-648-JIST or visit www.jist.com for a free catalog and more information.

Acquisitions Editor: Susan Pines
Development Editor: Jill Mazurczyk
Interior Designer: Aleata Howard
Cover Designer: Katy Bodenmiller
Interior Layout: Trudy Coler
Proofreader: Paula Lowell
Indexer: Tina Trettin

Printed in the United States of America
11 10 09 08 07   9 8 7 6 5 4 3 2

Library of Congress Cataloging-in-Publication Data

Shatkin, Laurence.
   90-minute college major matcher : choose your best major for a
great career / Laurence Shatkin.
      p. cm. -- (JIST's help in a hurry series)
   Includes index.
   ISBN-13: 978-1-59357-360-7 (alk. paper)
   ISBN-10: 1-59357-360-X (alk. paper)
   1. College majors. 2. Vocational guidance.   I. Title. II. Title:
Ninety minute college major matcher.
   LB2361.S366 2007
   378.1'99--dc22

                                        2006018664

All rights reserved. No part of this book may be reproduced in any form or by any means, or stored in a database or retrieval system, without prior written permission of the publisher except in the case of brief quotations embodied in articles or reviews. Making copies of any part of this book for any purpose other than your own personal use is a violation of United States copyright laws. For permission requests, please contact the Copyright Clearance Center at www.copyright.com or (978) 750-8400.

We have been careful to provide accurate information in this book, but it is possible that errors and omissions have been introduced. Please consider this in making any career plans or other important decisions. Trust your own judgment above all else and in all things.

Trademarks: All brand names and product names used in this book are trade names, service marks, trademarks, or registered trademarks of their respective owners.

ISBN 978-1-59357-360-7

Choose Your Major in 90 Minutes

Chances are that you're reading this book because you need to declare a major and you haven't yet made up your mind which one to choose. Or maybe you have chosen a major, but it isn't working out and you're thinking about choosing a new one. Perhaps you're not yet in college but you need to choose a major so you can decide on the best college for your education—or whether to go to college at all. Whatever your reason, you are facing a decision that every college student or college-bound student has to make sooner or later, and perhaps you feel paralyzed because it seems like such a big decision to make.

With the help that this book provides, you can follow a series of steps that will lead you to a rational decision, one based on careful consideration of your preferences and needs and on a thorough survey of the options available to you. Of course, no one resource can provide all the answers, but this book contains a wealth of facts and, more important, can prompt you to ask the right questions and then help you process the answers you get. And because you will be going about the process in a structured way, you will save precious time that could have been wasted in pursuing unanswerable questions or agonizing over decisions.

Yes, you really can make the choice in 90 minutes. Read "How You Can Benefit from This Book" on page viii for quick ways to use this small guide. Not everyone is that strapped for time, so this book will also be useful if you can devote more time to the decision.

Now get started on making a satisfying choice.

Contents

© JIST Works

A Brief Introduction to Using This Book

One of the reasons it's hard to choose a major is deciding where to start. Which comes first: choosing a college major or choosing a career? The truth is that this is a chicken-and-egg problem that people disagree about.

Some people say that first you should decide what career you want to pursue, then choose a major that helps you prepare for it. They tell you success stories about students who graduated with degrees in accounting, computer science, or some other career-oriented major, then got high-paying, fast-track career offers from businesses. (Students tend to prefer this approach.)

Other people take the opposite approach. They say that first you should decide on a major you really love, then choose a career that can take advantage of what you've learned. They tell you horror stories about students who declared a major in a career-oriented field such as engineering or business, only to discover that the coursework was so boring that they dropped out of college or changed majors and delayed graduation by one or more years. (Academic advisors tend to prefer this approach.)

Both approaches have elements of truth. And *the reason this book is so special* is that it lets you choose a four-year college major and a career *simultaneously*, instead of considering just one or the other. It links 120 majors to 257 careers. It informs you about what the career is like, and also about what you would study in the major. It tells you which careers are commonly associated with the major, and in some cases how graduates may go into careers in unexpected fields. And it is a college major *matcher* because it helps you identify majors and careers that are a good fit with your personal needs and preferences.

So the choice is yours: You can sign up for an expensive battery of personality tests and counseling sessions; you can dig through piles of college catalogs, examining and comparing the requirements for the majors; you can search through massive databases of career information, taking pains to determine the skill requirements and the income you can expect—or you can use this book to obtain self-understanding and get concise and authoritative facts about majors and careers that might suit you.

If the choice is not obvious already, turn to chapter 2 and start the exercises. You'll be surprised by how quickly you'll start seeing the connections between who you are and where you want to go.

What's in This Book?

This book is set up so that you can find information quickly, in a variety of ways. The first chapter clarifies what majors, minors, and concentrations are and discusses some important factors to consider as part of your decision. Chapters 2 through 4 offer paper-and-pencil exercises to help you decide what you want to get from your major and career. Based on these exercises, you'll assemble a Hot List of majors in chapter 5. Chapter 6 lets you browse descriptions of college majors and related careers, with 120 college majors arranged in alphabetical order.

How You Can Benefit from This Book

This isn't the only book about careers or college majors, but it is specially designed to knit the two tightly together so that you can decide about both at the same time. You can benefit from using the book in the following ways:

- Do the quick exercises in chapters 2 through 4 to help you zero in on what is most important to you in a major and a career. Tables and worksheets that accompany the exercises will help you assemble a "Hot List" in chapter 5, highlighting the majors and careers that may offer what you want.

- Browse chapter 6 for quick and effective information. This is easy because the description of each major begins with a brief definition of the major, followed by a table containing the facts about jobs that are related to the major.

- See specific and up-to-date facts about careers in chapter 6, derived from the databases of the U.S. Department of Labor.

- Easily compare majors and careers in chapter 6 with the consistent naming scheme used for work-related skills, values, and work conditions (derived from the Department of Labor's O*NET database). "O*NET" is the U.S. Department of Labor's Occupational Information Network database of career information.

- Quickly locate more information sources via the Classification of Instructional Programs (CIP) number that appears in the first paragraph of each major in chapter 6. This number links the college major to the standard coding scheme used for majors. The occupation names listed under "Related Jobs" are also standard titles that you can research elsewhere. This book can serve as a jumping-off point for consulting other reference works.

© JIST Works

Sources of This Information

The information in this book comes from the best and most current sources available.

Department of Labor's O*NET Database

The U.S. Department of Labor (DOL) is the nation's number-one source of information about careers. This book draws on release 9 of the DOL's O*NET database for ratings of occupational features—interests, skills, values satisfactions, and work conditions—that serve as the basis for assigning majors to the tables in chapters 2 and 3 and for describing the majors in chapter 6. For each feature, a score is calculated based on the difference between the occupation's O*NET rating on the level of that feature and the average rating for all occupations on the same feature. Then a weighted average of scores is computed, representing each of the jobs linked to the major in proportion to the size of its workforce. Finally, all the features in a domain (e.g., all skills) are put in descending order of their weighted averages, and the top five are selected for inclusion in the chapter 6 description. In the case of interests, only three are listed, or fewer if the first- or second-rated interest has a score much higher than the next-lowest interest.

A crosswalk table from the DOL identifies which careers are associated with each major. The information regarding average earnings in the careers is from the DOL's office of Occupational Employment Statistics and applies to November 2004. The information about job growth and openings in a career is based on the most recent data from another office of the DOL, Employment Projections, and it applies to the years from 2004 to 2014. Finally, much of the information about career paths and opportunities is from the DOL's best-selling *Occupational Outlook Handbook*. Taken together, these facts give you a good introduction to the wide range of careers linked to the majors in this book.

College Catalogs

The information for the "Typical Sequence of College Courses" is derived from research in actual college catalogs. For each major, I examined and compared several catalogs and identified commonly required courses. You may notice some variation in the number of courses listed. Some majors have fairly standard requirements that can be listed in detail; in some cases, a professional association mandates that certain courses be included. For other majors, notably the interdisciplinary subjects, requirements are either so minimal or so varied that it is difficult to list more than a handful of typical courses.

The "Typical Sequence of High School Courses" sections are based on a general understanding of which high school courses are considered prerequisites for the college-level courses required by the major. Consider these as suggestions, because often they are helpful for entering the major but are not required.

Final Points

When you read the information in this book about a major or career, keep in mind that the description covers what is *average* or *typical*—but in the real world plenty of exceptions exist. For example, one college may offer a major with an unusual emphasis not mentioned here. The earnings figures are national averages, so you may find different figures for income where you live. And if you start looking at "help wanted" advertisements, you may learn about jobs that require a somewhat different mix of skills than the ones listed here. Use this book as an introduction to the majors and careers. When you've found some choices that interest you, explore them in greater detail. You may be able to find a way to carve out a niche within a major or career to suit your particular abilities and interests.

Dedication

To Nancy Decker Shatkin, a onetime English major whose price is far above rubies.

Acknowledgments

This book owes much of its quality and usefulness to the suggestions of Susan Pines. Michael Farr provided an inspiring model with his Help in a Hurry books. John Liptak's comments on a previous book helped improve this one. The editing done by Jill Mazurczyk helped polish off some rough edges.

© JIST Works

Chapter 1

The Parts of a Major Decision

D eciding on a major is a big step, but you may be relieved to know that you're not signing your life away when you decide. Most majors allow some flexibility to tailor your classes to your particular interests. And if the major doesn't work out for you, you can switch majors at a later time. Let's begin the process of decision making by looking at what some of your options are.

What Is a Major?

A college major is an organized program of study with some specific requirements that you must complete. Usually the program of study focuses on a subject, and the academic requirements are designed so that you gain some in-depth knowledge of that subject. Typically the subject that is the focus of the major is the same as the department offering the major (e.g., accounting, English, chemistry, or sociology), but many colleges offer interdisciplinary majors, such as American Studies, that bridge several departments. Even majors that are aligned with a specific department have requirements from other departments to help you understand your main focus of interest. If the goal of the major is to prepare you for a specific career that you can pursue once you have your degree in hand, the major often includes a certain amount of supervised work experience. Majors that are less career-oriented and more academically oriented often include at least one course on research methods.

Some colleges offer majors with names such as "General Studies" that have few specific requirements. But, as most students do, this book focuses on the connection between majors and careers, and, therefore, most of the majors described here have required courses that equip you with knowledge and skills that you'll use on the job.

Four-year colleges typically require you to declare your major by the end of your sophomore year, but you should start thinking about your choice even before you apply to college. You may need to state your intended major when you apply for admission to college. And having some idea of your intended major may also help you decide on a college, because many majors are taught considerably better at some colleges than at others. For the particular major you have in mind, one college may have more experienced instructors, more course offerings, better access to instructors, major requirements better suited to careers, better-equipped labs, better library collections, better academic advisors, or better connections with employers.

Another reason to plan your major before you are required to declare it is that some majors are not open to just anyone who expresses interest. They may have specific entry requirements that you need to complete in high school and during your first two years of college, and there may even be competition for entry, meaning that your grades have to be better than simply getting by.

What About Concentrations, Minors, and Double Majors?

Majors that are highly career-oriented may give you few opportunities to choose courses that reflect your interests. For example, in some health care fields a professional association or licensing requirements mandate most of the courses you'll take.

In most majors, however, you can select courses to emphasize an aspect of the subject that interests you—such as ancient history as opposed to modern; nuclear physics as opposed to optics; or international business management as opposed to domestic. Sometimes the department sets the course requirements for the major to reflect two or more possible "concentrations" or "tracks." For each major included in chapter 6, you can find some of the most popular concentrations listed under the topic Specializations in the Major. Obviously your career goal is an important consideration when you choose a concentration within a major.

Of course, it is possible that you have a special interest that is not well represented by any of the concentrations in the major. For example, you might be interested in geology and dismayed to discover that the department does not have a concentration in French. In that case, you may consider doing a minor in the second subject or a double major in the two subjects.

Concentrations

A concentration within a major is not simply a matter of which courses you take within the department offering the major. Often a concentration will

© JIST Works

lead you to take appropriate supporting courses in other departments. For example, an economics major who concentrates in econometrics will probably take additional courses offered by the mathematics and computer science departments, whereas one who concentrates in applied economics will probably take additional business courses.

Students who have a very clear idea of their career goals may create do-it-yourself concentrations by choosing appropriate courses from departments outside their major. For example, a religious studies major who intends to do missionary work in Latin America may take courses in Spanish and Latin American history. A human resources major who intends to do industrial training may take courses in educational psychology.

Minors

If you have a strong interest in some area outside the department of your major, you may be able to *minor* in that other subject. A minor is a set of course requirements that amount to less than a major but that still put you on record as having some depth of knowledge of that field. By combining a major and a minor, you may create a particular niche for yourself in the working world that makes you attractive to employers. For example, with a major in chemistry and a minor in business, you may be a strong candidate for a sales job with a pharmaceuticals company. With a major in journalism and a minor in physics, you may become the science writer for a newspaper.

Double Majors

In some cases, it may be possible to pursue a double major—that is, to complete the requirements for two majors. This is most feasible when both majors do not load your schedule with large numbers of required courses. If both majors allow for many freely chosen courses (these are called "electives"), you may be able to satisfy the requirements for both.

Some people combine interests by studying one subject in college and a different one in graduate or professional school. For example, most social workers and librarians are expected to enter the workforce with a master's degree, but master's programs in social work do not require you to major in the same subject as an undergraduate, and master's programs in library science actively discourage it. Medical schools require applicants to have completed certain science and math courses as undergraduates, but it is possible to fit these courses into many majors, and a well-rounded academic background may give you an advantage over other applicants.

The lesson to take away is that a major does not need to be a straitjacket that confines you to one subject. So if you're nervous about declaring a major partly because you have a variety of interests, try to find creative ways to tailor your major. Look at the college catalog to see what concentrations are available and how much freedom you will have to take electives. Talk to an academic advisor about options for minors, double majors, or graduate study.

Customize Your Major

If you have a special interest, you may even be able to design your own major or minor in consultation with your academic advisor. Will Shortz, now the puzzle editor at the *New York Times,* designed a major in "enigmatology" (the study of puzzles) when he was an undergraduate at Indiana University, Bloomington. Obviously, nobody's going to let you major in "partyology." But if you can devise a program of study that will gain you in-depth knowledge of a particular field that is not covered well by any one department in your college, and if you can develop standards for measuring your progress in learning this field, perhaps you and your academic advisor can persuade the appropriate dean to recognize your program of study as a major.

Changing Majors

For one reason or another, you may decide later that you need to change your major. For example, you may earn poor grades in the major because the subject is either harder that you expected or so uninteresting that you aren't really trying to do the work. Or perhaps a course you take in a different field or a new career goal you learn about may capture your interest and lure you away from your original major. Keep in mind that unless the new major has requirements that are very similar to those of your original major, making this change is likely to set back your graduation date by one or more years. The sooner in your college career you decide to make the change, the less ground you'll lose, so ask your academic advisor to suggest a course that represents your intended major well and is not watered-down (e.g., Biology with Lab versus Biology for Poets), and take this course sooner rather than later.

The good news is that if you do the exercises in this book honestly and with an open mind, you can focus on the factors that are likely to make you want to stick with your choice of a major.

© JIST Works

Factors That Should Be Part of the Decision

The goal of this book is to help you choose a major and a career simultaneously, and to make your choice one that offers the best chances of satisfying you. You'll go through a series of exercises to clarify your **interests, skills, and favorite high school course**s. All of these are important factors in the decision—but before you look at those concerns, here are some other factors you'll probably want to consider.

Time and Expense Required

Some of the majors included in this book take longer than others to bear fruit as a career. People seeking careers in medicine, law, optometry, pharmacy, veterinary medicine, and (sometimes) clergy must complete years of postgraduate study and on-the-job training to earn professional status. These jobs tend to pay well or (in the case of clergy) have other outstanding rewards, but before you commit yourself to pursue one of these career goals, you have to be sure you have the determination and ability to go through the long preparatory process. The same is true of careers such as college teaching that require a master's or doctoral degree. You need to be confident that you will enjoy the major itself, not just the rewards at the end of the road, because it will be a long road, and college tuition keeps getting more and more expensive.

Some of the careers listed here require more than just a degree. For managerial jobs in particular, college graduates are expected to gain some experience in the workplace, learn the language of the industry, acquire people skills that usually aren't taught in college classrooms, and demonstrate their readiness through some temporary managerial assignments. Don't plan on a managerial career unless you are willing to pay your dues as a management trainee.

In some cases, a career linked to one of these majors may not actually require four years of college. For example, this book includes Agricultural Technicians, Food Science Technicians, Chemical Technicians, and several other technician-level jobs that you can enter with an associate degree. Some other jobs, such as Cost Estimators, Food Service Managers, Fish and Game Wardens, and Sketch Artists, are open to people who have gained work experience in related occupations or who get long-term on-the-job training. For these jobs a college education is not always necessary, but the degree may save you considerable time in getting ahead and may pave the way to further advancement or career shifts not open to those who lack the degree.

The time and expense of getting a college degree can also pay off later in ways that have nothing to do with your career. What you have learned in college may enable you to appreciate a well-designed building, an outstanding movie, or a nature walk better than someone without that background. A vacation in a foreign country, a story on the evening news, or a conversation with a stranger may connect with things you have learned in your major so that the experience is much more meaningful.

Competition

Rewarding careers often attract large numbers of job-seekers. The competition can begin in college or, for some careers, even earlier. As part of the decision about a major and a career, you need to get a realistic sense of your chances of entering and succeeding in the job.

This book can help give you an idea of the competition you'll face for jobs because, wherever possible, the descriptions of majors give indications of the job opportunities in the associated careers. In the Career Snapshots you'll notice statements such as "Competition is expected to be keen" or "Job opportunities are expected to be good." Another clue may be found in the information about how fast an occupation is growing and how many job openings are expected. But keep in mind that these nuggets of information are national averages. At the local level you may find either greater or less competition, so you need to investigate conditions where you plan to seek employment. People who do the hiring or have recently been employed can supply useful insights.

If you are already enrolled in college, you may get some answers from the staff of the career development office or from experienced faculty in the major you are considering. If you are not yet enrolled in college, consider that what recruiters tell you may be slanted as a sales pitch. Confirm what you hear by asking other sources, such as recent graduates, and be sure to ask about the college's recent job-placement track record for your intended major.

Of course, you may face competition long before you hit the job market. Some majors limit the number of people who enroll and admit only high-performing students. If you pursue a graduate or professional degree, expect

© JIST Works

competition for entry. Professional schools generally create a climate where, once admitted, students work hard but can expect to complete their degree (although often they compete for the best job prospects); many graduate departments, on the other hand, limit the number of students who are allowed to proceed beyond the master's degree into the doctoral program. Graduate students also compete for financial aid, such as fellowships that may pay a stipend.

So as you make plans, you need to decide whether you have the drive and the ability to withstand the competition that you will face. Talk to people currently in the program and measure your past grades and test scores against their backgrounds. Ask people in the workforce what it takes to succeed. If you expect a small but significant possibility of failure, consider how well you accept risk and construct an alternative plan in case your original goal does not work out. Many people have found success and happiness in their "plan-B" careers.

Key Points: Chapter 1

- A major focuses on a particular subject, but often you can pursue an additional interest through a concentration, a minor, a double major, or graduate study.

- You need to focus on not just the career goal, but also the time and expense that the major will require to reach that goal. Be honest about your commitment to the major.

- Don't forget to consider the amount of competition you will face for entering the major, succeeding in it, and entering the workforce. Everyone needs a dream, but also a realistic plan for reaching it.

Chapter 2

What Are Your Interests?

Before you can figure out where you're going, it helps to understand who you are. With the help of some quick and easy exercises in this chapter and the two that follow, you'll take a look at yourself and what matters most to you. You'll examine your priorities from several different angles:

- Your interests
- Your favorite high school courses
- Your skills

Each time you draw conclusions about your priorities, you'll get immediate feedback in terms of **college majors** and **related careers** that you should consider.

Then in "**Your Hot List of College Majors and Careers**" in chapter 5 you'll put together the suggestions from all three factors to create a Hot List of college majors that you should explore in chapter 6.

Your Interests: The Six Holland Types

Surely you have been in a situation where you attended an event, switched to a TV channel, or picked up a piece of reading matter that you found boring—knowing all the while that other people found it fascinating.

Tip: *As you do the exercises, keep in mind that for exercises about career planning there are no "right" or "wrong" answers. The most important thing they require is honesty.*

Different people have different interests. Becoming aware of your interests is an important first step in career planning. If your work tasks, work settings, and the information you use on the job are interesting to you, you are more likely to be happy and successful in your job.

One of the most useful ways of looking at work-related interests is in the terms that were developed by the researcher John L. Holland in the early 1950s. Analyzing the results of interest inventories, Holland found it helpful for people to compare themselves to six major interest types that he devised. (The Holland types are often referred to as *personality* types because they are sometimes applied to more than just career choice. But for the purposes of this book we're going to discuss them as interests.)

The terms Holland used for his six types may not be immediately clear to you when you first encounter them. That's why it helps to read these definitions:

The Holland Types Defined	
Interest	*Definition*
Realistic	Realistic occupations frequently involve work activities that include practical, hands-on problems and solutions. They often deal with plants, animals, and real-world materials like wood, tools, and machinery. Many of the occupations require working outside and do not involve a lot of paperwork or working closely with others.
Investigative	Investigative occupations frequently involve working with ideas and require an extensive amount of thinking. These occupations can involve searching for facts and figuring out problems mentally.
Artistic	Artistic occupations frequently involve working with forms, designs, and patterns. They often require self-expression and the work can be done without following a clear set of rules.
Social	Social occupations frequently involve working with, communicating with, and teaching people. These occupations often involve helping or providing service to others.
Enterprising	Enterprising occupations frequently involve starting up and carrying out projects. These occupations can involve leading people and making many decisions. They sometimes require risk taking and often deal with business.
Conventional	Conventional occupations frequently involve following set procedures and routines. These occupations can include working with data and details more than with ideas. Usually there is a clear line of authority to follow.

Holland demonstrated the relationships among these interest types by arranging them on a hexagon:

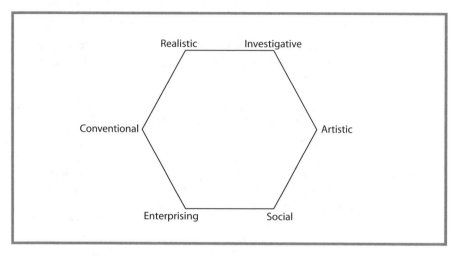

(After Holland, A Theory of Vocational Choice, 1959.)

Holland used this diagram to explain that people tend to have one dominant interest but may also be interested in one or more other types, and these usually are types that are adjacent to the dominant interest on the hexagon. Each interest type tends to have little in common with the interests on the opposite side of the hexagon. Therefore, for example, a person might have primarily Social interests, with an additional but smaller amount of Enterprising interests. Such a person's interests would be described by the two-letter code SE and might point this person toward work as an Employment Interviewer or a Security Guard (both coded SE). This person would probably have little interest in Realistic matters and likely would not be very happy or productive as a Civil Engineer (coded RI).

Perhaps you already know what Holland types describe you best, either based on the earlier definitions or because you have taken an assessment that has had its results reported as Holland types. If so, you can skip the next section and go to "Relating Interest Types to College Majors and Careers" on page 12. But if you are not clear about how to characterize your interests in Holland's terms, try the following exercise.

© JIST Works

Interests Checklist

The following checklist contains Holland's six work-related interest types and examples of activities for each. Think about which interest type includes one or more activities that have the greatest appeal to you. Keep in mind that these are only *examples,* not an exhaustive list of every activity of that type. You may know you are greatly interested in an activity of this type that is not listed among the examples. (For example, you may be interested in an art form not listed under Artistic.) Similarly, you can choose an interest type as the one that describes you even if you're not interested in *all* the activities listed. Many people have diverse interests; feel free to choose one or two types that might be of secondary interest to you.

In the blank spaces to the left, write a "1" to indicate your dominant interest type. You may also write a "2" or "3" to indicate other interest types that feature activities that interest you, but not as much as your principal type.

INTERESTS CHECKLIST

___ **Realistic:** Putting out forest fires; laying brick or tile; growing Christmas trees in a nursery; testing the quality of parts before shipment; enforcing fish and game laws; refinishing furniture; applying pesticides and fertilizers to plants.

___ **Investigative:** Making a map of the bottom of an ocean; determining the infection rate of a new disease; investigating crimes; studying the governments of different countries; inventing a replacement for sugar; diagnosing and treating sick animals; studying ways to reduce water pollution.

___ **Artistic:** Playing a musical instrument; creating special effects for movies; writing reviews of books or plays; dancing in a Broadway show; designing artwork for magazines; announcing a radio show; painting sets for plays.

___ **Social:** Teaching children how to read; helping people with family-related problems; organizing activities at a recreational facility; working with juveniles on probation; helping disabled people improve their skills for daily living; helping conduct a group therapy session; teaching children how to play sports.

(continued)

(continued)

_____ **Enterprising:** Giving a presentation about a product you are selling; managing a department within a large company; marketing a new line of clothing; negotiating business contracts; selling houses; managing the operations of a hotel; buying and selling stocks and bonds.

_____ **Conventional:** Organizing and scheduling office meetings; inventorying supplies using a hand-held computer; taking notes during a meeting; developing a spreadsheet using computer software; assisting senior-level accountants in performing bookkeeping tasks; maintaining employee records; using a word processor to edit and format documents.

Relating Interest Types to College Majors and Careers

Now that you have clarified where your work-related interests lie, it's time to consider majors and careers that will give you chances to pursue these interests. The following table lists the majors and careers included in this book that are associated with each of the six interest types. Most of the majors have two- or three-letter codes, meaning that they may be able to satisfy one or two secondary interests as well as a dominant interest.

Note that each major is given interest codes based on the *careers that the major is linked to,* and not necessarily on what you focus on while you are studying the major in college. For example, the American Studies major is listed in the Social interest type (with the code SIA) because the major is linked to the job *Area, Ethnic, and Cultural Studies Teachers, Postsecondary* (also coded SIA). Like most teaching jobs, this one involves a lot of working with and helping people and, therefore, is associated primarily with the Social interest type. While you are pursuing an American Studies major in college, however, you may have limited opportunities to work with and help people. In more career-oriented majors, such as Art (Artistic), Dietetics (Investigative), or Animal Science (Realistic), the activities you engage in as an undergraduate may more often reflect the experience of the job.

Also consider that some people with diverse interests choose majors that are not directly linked to their career goals. For example, a person with Enterprising interests might major in Russian (classified as Artistic) while intending to pursue a career in international sales; this person could take

© JIST Works

some business courses in college and learn the rest of the job through on-the-job training. Other people with diverse interests complete a minor related to their secondary interest field. Still others study one thing as an undergraduate and something else in graduate or professional school—or pursue a secondary interest as a hobby at the end of the workday.

With these considerations in mind, browse the following table to find majors and careers associated with your dominant interest type and perhaps with one or more secondary interest types. Write these in the blank spaces in the worksheet that follows the table on page 26, "College Majors and Careers That Relate to My Interests."

Interest Types and Related College Majors and Careers

Interest Type: REALISTIC

INTEREST TYPE(S): R   **RELATED MAJOR:** Agricultural Business and Economics

RELATED CAREERS AND THEIR INTEREST TYPES: Purchasing Agents and Buyers, Farm Products (ECR), First-Line Supervisors and Manager/Supervisors—Agricultural Crop Workers (ER), Nursery and Greenhouse Managers (ERC), Fish Hatchery Managers (ERC), Agricultural Crop Farm Managers (ERC), Agricultural Sciences Teachers, Postsecondary (IS), Nonfarm Animal Caretakers (R), Graders and Sorters, Agricultural Products (RC), Pest Control Workers (RC), First-Line Supervisors and Manager/Supervisors—Logging Workers (RE), Farmers and Ranchers (REC), Farm and Home Management Advisors (SRE)

INTEREST TYPE(S): REC   **RELATED MAJOR:** Mechanical Engineering

RELATED CAREERS AND THEIR INTEREST TYPES: Cost Estimators (CE), Engineering Managers (ERI), Engineering Teachers, Postsecondary (IRS), Mechanical Engineers (RI)

INTEREST TYPE(S): REI   **RELATED MAJOR:** Agronomy and Crop Science

RELATED CAREERS AND THEIR INTEREST TYPES: First-Line Supervisors and Manager/Supervisors—Agricultural Crop Workers (ER), Agricultural Crop Farm Managers (ERC), Plant Scientists (IR), Agricultural Sciences Teachers, Postsecondary (IS), Farmers and Ranchers (REC)

INTEREST TYPE(S): REI   **RELATED MAJOR:** Animal Science

RELATED CAREERS AND THEIR INTEREST TYPES: First-Line Supervisors and Manager/Supervisors—Animal Husbandry Workers (ER), Agricultural Crop Farm Managers (ERC), Animal Scientists (IR), Agricultural Sciences Teachers, Postsecondary (IS), Farmers and Ranchers (REC), First-Line Supervisors and Manager/Supervisors—Animal Care Workers, Except Livestock (RES), Food Science Technicians (RIC), Agricultural Technicians (RIC), Farm and Home Management Advisors (SRE)

(continued)

R=Realistic; I=Investigative; A=Artistic; S=Social; E=Enterprising; C=Conventional

(continued)

INTEREST TYPE(S): RES   **RELATED MAJOR:** Criminal Justice/Law Enforcement

RELATED CAREERS AND THEIR INTEREST TYPES: Immigration and Customs Inspectors (CER), Police Identification and Records Officers (CR), Criminal Investigators and Special Agents (EI), Police Detectives (ES), Child Support, Missing Persons, and Unemployment Insurance Fraud Investigators (ESC), Private Detectives and Investigators (ESR), Highway Patrol Pilots (RE), Bailiffs (SEC), Sheriffs and Deputy Sheriffs (SER), Police Patrol Officers (SRE)

INTEREST TYPE(S): RI   **RELATED MAJOR:** Forestry

RELATED CAREERS AND THEIR INTEREST TYPES: Range Managers (IR), Soil Conservationists (IRC), Foresters (RI), Forest and Conservation Workers (RI), Park Naturalists (SR)

INTEREST TYPE(S): RIC   **RELATED MAJOR:** Food Science

RELATED CAREERS AND THEIR INTEREST TYPES: Food Scientists and Technologists (IR), Agricultural Sciences Teachers, Postsecondary (IS), Food Science Technicians (RIC), Chemical Technicians (RIC), Agricultural Technicians (RIC)

INTEREST TYPE(S): RIE   **RELATED MAJOR:** Civil Engineering

RELATED CAREERS AND THEIR INTEREST TYPES: Engineering Managers (ERI), Engineering Teachers, Postsecondary (IRS), Civil Engineers (RI)

Interest Type: INVESTIGATIVE

INTEREST TYPE(S): I   **RELATED MAJOR:** Biochemistry

RELATED CAREERS AND THEIR INTEREST TYPES: Natural Sciences Managers (IE), Biochemists (IR), Medical Scientists, Except Epidemiologists (IRS), Biological Science Teachers, Postsecondary (IS)

INTEREST TYPE(S): I   **RELATED MAJOR:** Microbiology

RELATED CAREERS AND THEIR INTEREST TYPES: Natural Sciences Managers (IE), Microbiologists (IR), Medical Scientists, Except Epidemiologists (IRS), Biological Science Teachers, Postsecondary (IS)

INTEREST TYPE(S): I   **RELATED MAJOR:** Oceanography

RELATED CAREERS AND THEIR INTEREST TYPES: Natural Sciences Managers (IE), Geologists (IR), Hydrologists (IR), Biological Science Teachers, Postsecondary (IS)

INTEREST TYPE(S): I   **RELATED MAJOR:** Zoology

RELATED CAREERS AND THEIR INTEREST TYPES: Natural Sciences Managers (IE), Zoologists and Wildlife Biologists (IR), Biological Science Teachers, Postsecondary (IS)

R=Realistic; I=Investigative; A=Artistic; S=Social; E=Enterprising; C=Conventional

© JIST Works

INTEREST TYPE(S): IAS   **RELATED MAJOR:** History

RELATED CAREERS AND THEIR INTEREST TYPES: Curators (AI), Museum Technicians and Conservators (AR), Historians (IA), Archivists (IC), History Teachers, Postsecondary (SIA)

INTEREST TYPE(S): IAS   **RELATED MAJOR:** Urban Studies

RELATED CAREERS AND THEIR INTEREST TYPES: Sociologists (IAS)

INTEREST TYPE(S): IC   **RELATED MAJOR:** Mathematics

RELATED CAREERS AND THEIR INTEREST TYPES: Statisticians (IC), Natural Sciences Managers (IE), Mathematical Science Teachers, Postsecondary (ISC)

INTEREST TYPE(S): IC   **RELATED MAJOR:** Statistics

RELATED CAREERS AND THEIR INTEREST TYPES: Statisticians (IC), Natural Sciences Managers (IE), Mathematical Science Teachers, Postsecondary (ISC)

INTEREST TYPE(S): ICR   **RELATED MAJOR:** Management Information Systems

RELATED CAREERS AND THEIR INTEREST TYPES: Computer and Information Systems Managers (ECI), Database Administrators (ICR), Computer Programmers (IRC)

INTEREST TYPE(S): ICR   **RELATED MAJOR:** Pharmacy

RELATED CAREERS AND THEIR INTEREST TYPES: Pharmacists (ICR), Health Specialties Teachers, Postsecondary (IS)

INTEREST TYPE(S): IEC   **RELATED MAJOR:** Economics

RELATED CAREERS AND THEIR INTEREST TYPES: Economists (IEC), Market Research Analysts (IEC), Economics Teachers, Postsecondary (SIA)

INTEREST TYPE(S): IER   **RELATED MAJOR:** Astronomy

RELATED CAREERS AND THEIR INTEREST TYPES: Natural Sciences Managers (IE), Astronomers (IRC), Physicists (IRC)

INTEREST TYPE(S): IR   **RELATED MAJOR:** Environmental Science

RELATED CAREERS AND THEIR INTEREST TYPES: Environmental Science and Protection Technicians, Including Health (IR), Environmental Scientists and Specialists, Including Health (IR)

INTEREST TYPE(S): IR   **RELATED MAJOR:** Geography

RELATED CAREERS AND THEIR INTEREST TYPES: Geographers (IR)

INTEREST TYPE(S): IR   **RELATED MAJOR:** Optometry

RELATED CAREERS AND THEIR INTEREST TYPES: Optometrists (IR)

(continued)

R=Realistic; I=Investigative; A=Artistic; S=Social; E=Enterprising; C=Conventional

(continued)

INTEREST TYPE(S): IR   **RELATED MAJOR:** Soil Science

RELATED CAREERS AND THEIR INTEREST TYPES: Soil Scientists (IR), Microbiologists (IR), Biophysicists (IR), Biochemists (IR), Agricultural Sciences Teachers, Postsecondary (IS)

INTEREST TYPE(S): IR   **RELATED MAJOR:** Wildlife Management

RELATED CAREERS AND THEIR INTEREST TYPES: Range Managers (IR), Zoologists and Wildlife Biologists (IR), Soil Conservationists (IRC), Fish and Game Wardens (RIS), Park Naturalists (SR)

INTEREST TYPE(S): IRC   **RELATED MAJOR:** Chemistry

RELATED CAREERS AND THEIR INTEREST TYPES: Natural Sciences Managers (IE), Chemists (IRC), Chemistry Teachers, Postsecondary (ISR)

INTEREST TYPE(S): IRC   **RELATED MAJOR:** Computer Engineering

RELATED CAREERS AND THEIR INTEREST TYPES: Engineering Managers (ERI), Computer Hardware Engineers (IRC), Computer Software Engineers, Systems Software (IRC), Computer Software Engineers, Applications (IRC), Engineering Teachers, Postsecondary (IRS)

INTEREST TYPE(S): IRC   **RELATED MAJOR:** Computer Science

RELATED CAREERS AND THEIR INTEREST TYPES: Computer and Information Systems Managers (ECI), Computer Science Teachers, Postsecondary (IC), Database Administrators (ICR), Computer Software Engineers, Systems Software (IRC), Computer Software Engineers, Applications (IRC)

INTEREST TYPE(S): IRE   **RELATED MAJOR:** Aeronautical/Aerospace Engineering

RELATED CAREERS AND THEIR INTEREST TYPES: Engineering Managers (ERI), Aerospace Engineers (IR), Engineering Teachers, Postsecondary (IRS)

INTEREST TYPE(S): IRE   **RELATED MAJOR:** Electrical Engineering

RELATED CAREERS AND THEIR INTEREST TYPES: Engineering Managers (ERI), Electrical Engineers (IR), Electronics Engineers, Except Computer (IR), Engineering Teachers, Postsecondary (IRS)

INTEREST TYPE(S): IRE   **RELATED MAJOR:** Geology

RELATED CAREERS AND THEIR INTEREST TYPES: Natural Sciences Managers (IE), Hydrologists (IR), Geologists (IR)

INTEREST TYPE(S): IRE   **RELATED MAJOR:** Geophysics

RELATED CAREERS AND THEIR INTEREST TYPES: Natural Sciences Managers (IE), Geologists (IR)

INTEREST TYPE(S): IRE   **RELATED MAJOR:** Physics

RELATED CAREERS AND THEIR INTEREST TYPES: Natural Sciences Managers (IE), Physicists (IRC), Physics Teachers, Postsecondary (ISR)

R=Realistic; I=Investigative; A=Artistic; S=Social; E=Enterprising; C=Conventional

© JIST Works

INTEREST TYPE(S): IRS   **RELATED MAJOR:** Medical Technology

RELATED CAREERS AND THEIR INTEREST TYPES: Medical and Clinical Laboratory Technologists (IR), Health Specialties Teachers, Postsecondary (IS)

INTEREST TYPE(S): IS   **RELATED MAJOR:** Chiropractic

RELATED CAREERS AND THEIR INTEREST TYPES: Chiropractors (IRS), Health Specialties Teachers, Postsecondary (IS)

INTEREST TYPE(S): IS   **RELATED MAJOR:** Occupational Health and Industrial Hygiene

RELATED CAREERS AND THEIR INTEREST TYPES: Health Specialties Teachers, Postsecondary (IS), Occupational Health and Safety Specialists (SEI)

INTEREST TYPE(S): IS   **RELATED MAJOR:** Physician Assisting

RELATED CAREERS AND THEIR INTEREST TYPES: Health Specialties Teachers, Postsecondary (IS), Physician Assistants (IS)

INTEREST TYPE(S): IS   **RELATED MAJOR:** Speech-Language Pathology and Audiology

RELATED CAREERS AND THEIR INTEREST TYPES: Health Specialties Teachers, Postsecondary (IS), Speech-Language Pathologists (SI), Audiologists (SI)

INTEREST TYPE(S): ISA   **RELATED MAJOR:** Anthropology

RELATED CAREERS AND THEIR INTEREST TYPES: Anthropologists (ISA), Anthropology and Archeology Teachers, Postsecondary (SIA)

INTEREST TYPE(S): ISA   **RELATED MAJOR:** Archeology

RELATED CAREERS AND THEIR INTEREST TYPES: Archeologists (IR), Anthropology and Archeology Teachers, Postsecondary (SIA)

INTEREST TYPE(S): ISA   **RELATED MAJOR:** Political Science

RELATED CAREERS AND THEIR INTEREST TYPES: Political Scientists (IA), Political Science Teachers, Postsecondary (SIA)

INTEREST TYPE(S): ISA   **RELATED MAJOR:** Psychology

RELATED CAREERS AND THEIR INTEREST TYPES: Clinical Psychologists (IAS), Industrial-Organizational Psychologists (IEA), Educational Psychologists (IS), Psychology Teachers, Postsecondary (SIA), Counseling Psychologists (SIA)

INTEREST TYPE(S): ISE   **RELATED MAJOR:** Biology

RELATED CAREERS AND THEIR INTEREST TYPES: Natural Sciences Managers (IE), Biological Science Teachers, Postsecondary (IS)

(continued)

R=Realistic; I=Investigative; A=Artistic; S=Social; E=Enterprising; C=Conventional

(continued)

INTEREST TYPE(S): ISE   **RELATED MAJOR:** Botany

RELATED CAREERS AND THEIR INTEREST TYPES: Natural Sciences Managers (IE), Biological Science Teachers, Postsecondary (IS)

INTEREST TYPE(S): ISR   **RELATED MAJOR:** Dentistry

RELATED CAREERS AND THEIR INTEREST TYPES: Dentists, General (IRS), Health Specialties Teachers, Postsecondary (IS)

INTEREST TYPE(S): ISR   **RELATED MAJOR:** Dietetics

RELATED CAREERS AND THEIR INTEREST TYPES: Dietitians and Nutritionists (IES), Dietetic Technicians (SRI)

INTEREST TYPE(S): ISR   **RELATED MAJOR:** Medicine

RELATED CAREERS AND THEIR INTEREST TYPES: Obstetricians and Gynecologists (I), Pediatricians, General (I), Family and General Practitioners (I), Internists, General (I), Psychiatrists (IAS), Anesthesiologists (IR), Surgeons (IR)

INTEREST TYPE(S): ISR   **RELATED MAJOR:** Orthotics/Prosthetics

RELATED CAREERS AND THEIR INTEREST TYPES: Health Specialties Teachers, Postsecondary (IS), Medical Appliance Technicians (RI), Orthotists and Prosthetists (SIR)

INTEREST TYPE(S): ISR   **RELATED MAJOR:** Veterinary Medicine

RELATED CAREERS AND THEIR INTEREST TYPES: Veterinarians (IR), Health Specialties Teachers, Postsecondary (IS)

Interest Type: ARTISTIC

INTEREST TYPE(S): A   **RELATED MAJOR:** Industrial Design

RELATED CAREERS AND THEIR INTEREST TYPES: Graphic Designers (AE), Commercial and Industrial Designers (ARE), Art, Drama, and Music Teachers, Postsecondary (ASI)

INTEREST TYPE(S): AC   **RELATED MAJOR:** Library Science

RELATED CAREERS AND THEIR INTEREST TYPES: Librarians (AC)

INTEREST TYPE(S): AES   **RELATED MAJOR:** Drama/Theater Arts

RELATED CAREERS AND THEIR INTEREST TYPES: Producers (AE), Directors—Stage, Motion Pictures, Television, and Radio (AE), Talent Directors (AES), Art, Drama, and Music Teachers, Postsecondary (ASI), Program Directors (EA), Technical Directors/Managers (RAE)

INTEREST TYPE(S): AES   **RELATED MAJOR:** Film/Cinema Studies

RELATED CAREERS AND THEIR INTEREST TYPES: Film and Video Editors (A), Producers (AE), Directors—Stage, Motion Pictures, Television, and Radio (AE),

R=Realistic; I=Investigative; A=Artistic; S=Social; E=Enterprising; C=Conventional

© *JIST Works*

Talent Directors (AES), Camera Operators, Television, Video, and Motion Picture (AR), Art, Drama, and Music Teachers, Postsecondary (ASI), Program Directors (EA), Technical Directors/Managers (RAE)

INTEREST TYPE(S): AES **RELATED MAJOR:** Journalism and Mass Communications

RELATED CAREERS AND THEIR INTEREST TYPES: Copy Writers (AES), Reporters and Correspondents (AIE), Broadcast News Analysts (AS), Caption Writers (ASC), Editors (ASE)

INTEREST TYPE(S): ARI **RELATED MAJOR:** Architecture

RELATED CAREERS AND THEIR INTEREST TYPES: Architects, Except Landscape and Naval (ARI), Engineering Managers (ERI)

INTEREST TYPE(S): ARI **RELATED MAJOR:** Landscape Architecture

RELATED CAREERS AND THEIR INTEREST TYPES: Landscape Architects (ARI), Engineering Managers (ERI)

INTEREST TYPE(S): ASE **RELATED MAJOR:** Communications Studies/Speech

RELATED CAREERS AND THEIR INTEREST TYPES: Creative Writers (A), Copy Writers (AES), Writers and Authors (AI), Poets and Lyricists (AI), Caption Writers (ASC), Editors (ASE), Public Address System and Other Announcers (SAE)

INTEREST TYPE(S): ASI **RELATED MAJOR:** Art

RELATED CAREERS AND THEIR INTEREST TYPES: Art Directors (AE), Cartoonists (AE), Sculptors (AR), Sketch Artists (AR), Painters and Illustrators (AR), Art, Drama, and Music Teachers, Postsecondary (ASI)

INTEREST TYPE(S): ASI **RELATED MAJOR:** Art History

RELATED CAREERS AND THEIR INTEREST TYPES: Curators (AI), Museum Technicians and Conservators (AR), Art, Drama, and Music Teachers, Postsecondary (ASI), Archivists (IC)

INTEREST TYPE(S): ASI **RELATED MAJOR:** Chinese

RELATED CAREERS AND THEIR INTEREST TYPES: Interpreters and Translators (ASI), Foreign Language and Literature Teachers, Postsecondary (ASI)

INTEREST TYPE(S): ASI **RELATED MAJOR:** Classics

RELATED CAREERS AND THEIR INTEREST TYPES: Interpreters and Translators (ASI), Foreign Language and Literature Teachers, Postsecondary (ASI)

(continued)

R=Realistic; I=Investigative; A=Artistic; S=Social; E=Enterprising; C=Conventional

(continued)

INTEREST TYPE(S): ASI   **RELATED MAJOR:** Dance

RELATED CAREERS AND THEIR INTEREST TYPES: Choreographers (ASE), Art, Drama, and Music Teachers, Postsecondary (ASI)

INTEREST TYPE(S): ASI   **RELATED MAJOR:** English

RELATED CAREERS AND THEIR INTEREST TYPES: English Language and Literature Teachers, Postsecondary (ASI)

INTEREST TYPE(S): ASI   **RELATED MAJOR:** French

RELATED CAREERS AND THEIR INTEREST TYPES: Interpreters and Translators (ASI), Foreign Language and Literature Teachers, Postsecondary (ASI)

INTEREST TYPE(S): ASI   **RELATED MAJOR:** German

RELATED CAREERS AND THEIR INTEREST TYPES: Interpreters and Translators (ASI), Foreign Language and Literature Teachers, Postsecondary (ASI)

INTEREST TYPE(S): ASI   **RELATED MAJOR:** Interior Design

RELATED CAREERS AND THEIR INTEREST TYPES: Interior Designers (AE), Art, Drama, and Music Teachers, Postsecondary (ASI)

INTEREST TYPE(S): ASI   **RELATED MAJOR:** Japanese

RELATED CAREERS AND THEIR INTEREST TYPES: Interpreters and Translators (ASI), Foreign Language and Literature Teachers, Postsecondary (ASI)

INTEREST TYPE(S): ASI   **RELATED MAJOR:** Modern Foreign Language

RELATED CAREERS AND THEIR INTEREST TYPES: Foreign Language and Literature Teachers, Postsecondary (ASI), Interpreters and Translators (ASI)

INTEREST TYPE(S): ASI   **RELATED MAJOR:** Music

RELATED CAREERS AND THEIR INTEREST TYPES: Composers (A), Music Arrangers and Orchestrators (A), Music Directors (ASE), Art, Drama, and Music Teachers, Postsecondary (ASI)

INTEREST TYPE(S): ASI   **RELATED MAJOR:** Russian

RELATED CAREERS AND THEIR INTEREST TYPES: Interpreters and Translators (ASI), Foreign Language and Literature Teachers, Postsecondary (ASI)

INTEREST TYPE(S): ASI   **RELATED MAJOR:** Spanish

RELATED CAREERS AND THEIR INTEREST TYPES: Interpreters and Translators (ASI), Foreign Language and Literature Teachers, Postsecondary (ASI)

R=Realistic; I=Investigative; A=Artistic; S=Social; E=Enterprising; C=Conventional

© JIST Works

Interest Type: SOCIAL

INTEREST TYPE(S): S   **RELATED MAJOR:** Business Education

RELATED CAREERS AND THEIR INTEREST TYPES: Secondary School Teachers, Except Special and Vocational Education (SAI), Vocational Education Teachers, Postsecondary (SR)

INTEREST TYPE(S): S   **RELATED MAJOR:** Elementary Education

RELATED CAREERS AND THEIR INTEREST TYPES: Elementary School Teachers, Except Special Education (SAI)

INTEREST TYPE(S): S   **RELATED MAJOR:** Industrial/Technology Education

RELATED CAREERS AND THEIR INTEREST TYPES: Vocational Education Teachers, Middle School (SAI), Vocational Education Teachers, Secondary School (SAI)

INTEREST TYPE(S): S   **RELATED MAJOR:** Philosophy

RELATED CAREERS AND THEIR INTEREST TYPES: Clergy (SAE), Directors, Religious Activities and Education (SEA)

INTEREST TYPE(S): S   **RELATED MAJOR:** Physical Education

RELATED CAREERS AND THEIR INTEREST TYPES: Coaches and Scouts (ERS), Middle School Teachers, Except Special and Vocational Education (SAI), Secondary School Teachers, Except Special and Vocational Education (SAI), Fitness Trainers and Aerobics Instructors (SRE)

INTEREST TYPE(S): S   **RELATED MAJOR:** Social Work

RELATED CAREERS AND THEIR INTEREST TYPES: Child, Family, and School Social Workers (S), Probation Officers and Correctional Treatment Specialists (SC)

INTEREST TYPE(S): S   **RELATED MAJOR:** Special Education

RELATED CAREERS AND THEIR INTEREST TYPES: Special Education Teachers, Middle School (SA), Special Education Teachers, Secondary School (SA), Special Education Teachers, Preschool, Kindergarten, and Elementary School (SA)

INTEREST TYPE(S): SAE   **RELATED MAJOR:** Religion/Religious Studies

RELATED CAREERS AND THEIR INTEREST TYPES: Clergy (SAE)

INTEREST TYPE(S): SAI   **RELATED MAJOR:** Early Childhood Education

RELATED CAREERS AND THEIR INTEREST TYPES: Kindergarten Teachers, Except Special Education (SA), Preschool Teachers, Except Special Education (SA)

INTEREST TYPE(S): SAI   **RELATED MAJOR:** Humanities

RELATED CAREERS AND THEIR INTEREST TYPES: Art, Drama, and Music Teachers, Postsecondary (ASI), English Language and Literature Teachers, Postsecondary (ASI), Foreign Language and Literature Teachers, Postsecondary (ASI), Economics Teachers,

(continued)

R=Realistic; I=Investigative; A=Artistic; S=Social; E=Enterprising; C=Conventional

---

(continued)

Postsecondary (SIA), Psychology Teachers, Postsecondary (SIA), Area, Ethnic, and Cultural Studies Teachers, Postsecondary (SIA), Anthropology and Archeology Teachers, Postsecondary (SIA), Sociology Teachers, Postsecondary (SIA), Political Science Teachers, Postsecondary (SIA), History Teachers, Postsecondary (SIA), Graduate Teaching Assistants (SIC)

INTEREST TYPE(S): SAI **RELATED MAJOR:** Secondary Education

RELATED CAREERS AND THEIR INTEREST TYPES: Secondary School Teachers, Except Special and Vocational Education (SAI)

INTEREST TYPE(S): SAR **RELATED MAJOR:** Parks and Recreation Management

RELATED CAREERS AND THEIR INTEREST TYPES: Recreation Workers (SAR)

INTEREST TYPE(S): SEC **RELATED MAJOR:** Family and Consumer Sciences

RELATED CAREERS AND THEIR INTEREST TYPES: Technical Writers (ASE), Public Relations Specialists (EAS), Sales Managers (EC), Marketing Managers (EC), First-Line Supervisors/Managers of Retail Sales Workers (EC), Secondary School Teachers, Except Special and Vocational Education (SAI), Middle School Teachers, Except Special and Vocational Education (SAI), Farm and Home Management Advisors (SRE)

INTEREST TYPE(S): SEC **RELATED MAJOR:** Human Resources Management

RELATED CAREERS AND THEIR INTEREST TYPES: Personnel Recruiters (ES), Training and Development Managers (ESC), Compensation and Benefits Managers (ESC), Compensation, Benefits, and Job Analysis Specialists (ICE), Training and Development Specialists (SEC), Employment Interviewers, Private or Public Employment Service (SEC)

INTEREST TYPE(S): SI **RELATED MAJOR:** Nursing (R.N. Training)

RELATED CAREERS AND THEIR INTEREST TYPES: Registered Nurses (SI), Nursing Instructors and Teachers, Postsecondary (SI)

INTEREST TYPE(S): SI **RELATED MAJOR:** Podiatry

RELATED CAREERS AND THEIR INTEREST TYPES: Podiatrists (SI)

INTEREST TYPE(S): SIA **RELATED MAJOR:** African-American Studies

RELATED CAREERS AND THEIR INTEREST TYPES: Area, Ethnic, and Cultural Studies Teachers, Postsecondary (SIA)

INTEREST TYPE(S): SIA **RELATED MAJOR:** American Studies

RELATED CAREERS AND THEIR INTEREST TYPES: Area, Ethnic, and Cultural Studies Teachers, Postsecondary (SIA)

INTEREST TYPE(S): SIA **RELATED MAJOR:** Area Studies

RELATED CAREERS AND THEIR INTEREST TYPES: Area, Ethnic, and Cultural Studies Teachers, Postsecondary (SIA)

R=Realistic; I=Investigative; A=Artistic; S=Social; E=Enterprising; C=Conventional

© JIST Works

INTEREST TYPE(S): SIA   **RELATED MAJOR:** Sociology

RELATED CAREERS AND THEIR INTEREST TYPES: Sociologists (IAS), Sociology Teachers, Postsecondary (SIA)

INTEREST TYPE(S): SIA   **RELATED MAJOR:** Women's Studies

RELATED CAREERS AND THEIR INTEREST TYPES: Area, Ethnic, and Cultural Studies Teachers, Postsecondary (SIA)

INTEREST TYPE(S): SIR   **RELATED MAJOR:** Occupational Therapy

RELATED CAREERS AND THEIR INTEREST TYPES: Health Specialties Teachers, Postsecondary (IS), Occupational Therapists (SR)

INTEREST TYPE(S): SIR   **RELATED MAJOR:** Physical Therapy

RELATED CAREERS AND THEIR INTEREST TYPES: Health Specialties Teachers, Postsecondary (IS), Physical Therapists (SRI)

Interest Type: ENTERPRISING

INTEREST TYPE(S): E   **RELATED MAJOR:** Law

RELATED CAREERS AND THEIR INTEREST TYPES: Lawyers (EC), Law Clerks (ECS), Judges, Magistrate Judges, and Magistrates (ES), Arbitrators, Mediators, and Conciliators (ES), Administrative Law Judges, Adjudicators, and Hearing Officers (ES)

INTEREST TYPE(S): EAS   **RELATED MAJOR:** Advertising

RELATED CAREERS AND THEIR INTEREST TYPES: Advertising and Promotions Managers (AE), Advertising Sales Agents (ESC)

INTEREST TYPE(S): EAS   **RELATED MAJOR:** Public Relations

RELATED CAREERS AND THEIR INTEREST TYPES: Advertising and Promotions Managers (AE), Public Relations Specialists (EAS)

INTEREST TYPE(S): EC   **RELATED MAJOR:** Marketing

RELATED CAREERS AND THEIR INTEREST TYPES: Advertising and Promotions Managers (AE), Marketing Managers (EC), Sales Managers (EC)

INTEREST TYPE(S): ECR   **RELATED MAJOR:** Operations Management

RELATED CAREERS AND THEIR INTEREST TYPES: Industrial Production Managers (EC), Transportation Managers (EC), Computer and Information Systems Managers (ECI), Storage and Distribution Managers (ECR), First-Line Supervisors/Managers of Production and Operating Workers (ERC), Construction Managers (ERC), First-Line Supervisors/Managers of Mechanics, Installers, and Repairers (ERC)

(continued)

R=Realistic; I=Investigative; A=Artistic; S=Social; E=Enterprising; C=Conventional

(continued)

INTEREST TYPE(S): ECS   **RELATED MAJOR:** Business Management

RELATED CAREERS AND THEIR INTEREST TYPES: Cost Estimators (CE), Transportation Managers (EC), Industrial Production Managers (EC), Sales Managers (EC), Management Analysts (ECI), Storage and Distribution Managers (ECR), Administrative Services Managers (ECS), Private Sector Executives (ECS), Construction Managers (ERC), Social and Community Service Managers (SE)

INTEREST TYPE(S): ECS   **RELATED MAJOR:** Finance

RELATED CAREERS AND THEIR INTEREST TYPES: Budget Analysts (CE), Credit Analysts (CE), Treasurers, Controllers, and Chief Financial Officers (EC), Financial Managers, Branch or Department (ECS), Loan Officers (ESC), Financial Analysts (ICE), Personal Financial Advisors (SEC)

INTEREST TYPE(S): ECS   **RELATED MAJOR:** Insurance

RELATED CAREERS AND THEIR INTEREST TYPES: Insurance Underwriters (CE), Insurance Appraisers, Auto Damage (CRE), Wholesale and Retail Buyers, Except Farm Products (EC), Purchasing Agents, Except Wholesale, Retail, and Farm Products (EC), Telemarketers (ECS), Insurance Adjusters, Examiners, and Investigators (EI), Sales Representatives, Wholesale and Manufacturing, Except Technical and Scientific Products (ES), Insurance Sales Agents (ESC)

INTEREST TYPE(S): ECS   **RELATED MAJOR:** International Business

RELATED CAREERS AND THEIR INTEREST TYPES: Private Sector Executives (ECS)

INTEREST TYPE(S): ECS   **RELATED MAJOR:** International Relations

RELATED CAREERS AND THEIR INTEREST TYPES: Government Service Executives (ECS), Political Scientists (IA), Political Science Teachers, Postsecondary (SIA)

INTEREST TYPE(S): ECS   **RELATED MAJOR:** Public Administration

RELATED CAREERS AND THEIR INTEREST TYPES: Transportation Managers (EC), Storage and Distribution Managers (ECR), Administrative Services Managers (ECS), Postmasters and Mail Superintendents (ECS), Government Service Executives (ECS), Social and Community Service Managers (SE)

INTEREST TYPE(S): ECS   **RELATED MAJOR:** Transportation and Logistics Management

RELATED CAREERS AND THEIR INTEREST TYPES: Transportation Managers (EC), Storage and Distribution Managers (ECR), Administrative Services Managers (ECS)

INTEREST TYPE(S): EIR   **RELATED MAJOR:** Agricultural Engineering

RELATED CAREERS AND THEIR INTEREST TYPES: Engineering Managers (ERI), Agricultural Engineers (IR), Engineering Teachers, Postsecondary (IRS)

INTEREST TYPE(S): EIR   **RELATED MAJOR:** Bioengineering

RELATED CAREERS AND THEIR INTEREST TYPES: Engineering Managers (ERI), Agricultural Engineers (IR), Engineering Teachers, Postsecondary (IRS)

R=Realistic; I=Investigative; A=Artistic; S=Social; E=Enterprising; C=Conventional

© JIST Works

INTEREST TYPE(S): EIR   **RELATED MAJOR:** Chemical Engineering
RELATED CAREERS AND THEIR INTEREST TYPES: Engineering Managers (ERI), Chemical Engineers (IR), Engineering Teachers, Postsecondary (IRS)

INTEREST TYPE(S): EIR   **RELATED MAJOR:** Industrial Engineering
RELATED CAREERS AND THEIR INTEREST TYPES: Operations Research Analysts (ICR), Natural Sciences Managers (IE)

INTEREST TYPE(S): EIR   **RELATED MAJOR:** Materials Science
RELATED CAREERS AND THEIR INTEREST TYPES: Engineering Managers (ERI), Materials Scientists (IR), Engineering Teachers, Postsecondary (IRS)

INTEREST TYPE(S): EIR   **RELATED MAJOR:** Metallurgical Engineering
RELATED CAREERS AND THEIR INTEREST TYPES: Engineering Managers (ERI), Materials Engineers (IR), Engineering Teachers, Postsecondary (IRS)

INTEREST TYPE(S): EIR   **RELATED MAJOR:** Petroleum Engineering
RELATED CAREERS AND THEIR INTEREST TYPES: Engineering Managers (ERI), Engineering Teachers, Postsecondary (IRS), Petroleum Engineers (RI)

INTEREST TYPE(S): ES   **RELATED MAJOR:** Hospital/Health Facilities Administration
RELATED CAREERS AND THEIR INTEREST TYPES: Medical and Health Services Managers (ES)

INTEREST TYPE(S): ES   **RELATED MAJOR:** Health Information Systems Administration
RELATED CAREERS AND THEIR INTEREST TYPES: Medical and Health Services Managers (ES)

INTEREST TYPE(S): ESC   **RELATED MAJOR:** Hotel/Motel and Restaurant Management
RELATED CAREERS AND THEIR INTEREST TYPES: Lodging Managers (ECS), Food Service Managers (ECS), Residential Advisors (SC)

INTEREST TYPE(S): ESC   **RELATED MAJOR:** Industrial and Labor Relations
RELATED CAREERS AND THEIR INTEREST TYPES: Personnel Recruiters (ES), Compensation and Benefits Managers (ESC), Compensation, Benefits, and Job Analysis Specialists (ICE), Employment Interviewers, Private or Public Employment Service (SEC)

(continued)

R=Realistic; I=Investigative; A=Artistic; S=Social; E=Enterprising; C=Conventional

(continued)

Interest Type: CONVENTIONAL

INTEREST TYPE(S): CE   **RELATED MAJOR:** Accounting

RELATED CAREERS AND THEIR INTEREST TYPES: Tax Examiners, Collectors, and Revenue Agents (CE), Auditors (CE), Budget Analysts (CE), Credit Analysts (CE), Accountants (CE), Financial Examiners (EC)

INTEREST TYPE(S): CI   **RELATED MAJOR:** Actuarial Science

RELATED CAREERS AND THEIR INTEREST TYPES: Actuaries (CI)

Use the following worksheet to jot down the majors and careers that relate to your main interest or interests.

COLLEGE MAJORS AND CAREERS THAT RELATE TO MY INTERESTS

_____

_____

_____

_____

_____

_____

Key Points: Chapter 2

- People who do work that interests them tend to be happier and more successful.

- The six Holland types can provide a useful way of organizing work-related interests into a few large categories. Understanding your Holland type(s) can help you choose a major and a career.

- If you have diverse interests, it is possible to satisfy them by identifying a major that combines them or by rounding out a major with a minor, a graduate program, or an atypical career path.

© JIST Works

Chapter 3

What Are Your Skills?

D ifferent kinds of work demand different skills, and people vary in what skills they bring to the workplace. Most people want to go into a kind of work where they will be able to handle the skill requirements. Of course, you don't yet *have* all the skills you will need for your career—that's why you are planning to get further education. Nevertheless, based on your experience in school, you probably have a good idea of which skills you learn easily and which come harder. You may also have work experience that indicates some of your skills.

Skills Checklist

The following checklist defines 27 of the skills that the U.S. Department of Labor includes in the O*NET database. For each skill, ask yourself, "What things have I done in which I've used this skill *at a high level* and *enjoyed* using it?" If you can think of several good examples, mark the name of the skill with a plus sign in the blank space at the left; otherwise, move on to another skill.

Some people find it difficult to judge their own skills, so just do your best here.

SKILLS CHECKLIST

___ **Active Learning:** Understanding the implications of new information for both current and future problem-solving and decision-making.

___ **Active Listening:** Giving full attention to what other people are saying, taking time to understand the points being made, asking questions as appropriate, and not interrupting at inappropriate times.

___ **Complex Problem Solving:** Identifying complex problems and reviewing related information to develop and evaluate options and implement solutions.

(continued)

(continued)

___ **Coordination:** Adjusting actions in relation to others' actions.

___ **Critical Thinking:** Using logic and reasoning to identify the strengths and weaknesses of alternative solutions, conclusions, or approaches to problems.

___ **Instructing:** Teaching others how to do something.

___ **Judgment and Decision Making:** Considering the relative costs and benefits of potential actions to choose the most appropriate one.

___ **Learning Strategies:** Selecting and using training/instructional methods and procedures appropriate for the situation when learning or teaching new things.

___ **Management of Financial Resources:** Determining how money will be spent to get the work done and accounting for these expenditures.

___ **Management of Material Resources:** Obtaining and seeing to the appropriate use of equipment, facilities, and materials needed to do certain work.

___ **Management of Personnel Resources:** Motivating, developing, and directing people as they work; identifying the best people for the job.

___ **Mathematics:** Using mathematics to solve problems.

___ **Negotiation:** Bringing others together and trying to reconcile differences.

___ **Operation Monitoring:** Watching gauges, dials, or other indicators to make sure a machine is working properly.

___ **Operations Analysis:** Analyzing needs and product requirements to create a design.

___ **Persuasion:** Persuading others to change their minds or behavior.

___ **Programming:** Writing computer programs for various purposes.

___ **Reading Comprehension:** Understanding written sentences and paragraphs in work-related documents.

___ **Science:** Using scientific rules and methods to solve problems.

© JIST Works

___ **Service Orientation:** Actively looking for ways to help people.

___ **Social Perceptiveness:** Being aware of others' reactions and understanding why they react as they do.

___ **Speaking:** Talking to others to convey information effectively.

___ **Systems Evaluation:** Identifying measures or indicators of system performance and the actions needed to improve or correct performance relative to the goals of the system.

___ **Technology Design:** Generating or adapting equipment and technology to serve user needs.

___ **Time Management:** Managing one's own time and the time of others.

___ **Troubleshooting:** Determining causes of operating errors and deciding what to do about them.

___ **Writing:** Communicating effectively in writing as appropriate for the needs of the audience.

Now that you've looked at all the skills and marked those that you feel most positive about, go back and choose three skills that you would *most* like to use in your career. In the blank spaces to the left, write a "1," "2," and "3" to indicate your top three.

Relating Your Skills to College Majors and Careers

The following table relates these 27 skills to college majors and careers. Using the three skills that you marked in the Skills Checklist, find the corresponding college majors and careers and circle the ones that look particularly interesting to you.

Note: *When a list was very large, we limited it to the 20 highest-rated majors and their related careers.*

Skills and Related College Majors and Careers

Skill: ACTIVE LEARNING

RELATED MAJORS: Actuarial Science; Anthropology; Archeology; Astronomy; Biology; Botany; Chemistry; Geology; Geophysics; Mathematics; Oceanography; Physics; Statistics; Zoology

RELATED CAREERS: Actuaries; Anthropologists; Anthropology and Archeology Teachers, Postsecondary; Archeologists; Astronomers; Atmospheric, Earth, Marine, and Space Sciences Teachers, Postsecondary; Biological Science Teachers, Postsecondary; Chemistry Teachers, Postsecondary; Chemists; Geologists; Geoscientists, Except Hydrologists and Geographers; Hydrologists; Mathematical Science Teachers, Postsecondary; Mathematicians; Natural Sciences Managers; Physicists; Physics Teachers, Postsecondary; Statisticians; Zoologists and Wildlife Biologists

Skill: ACTIVE LISTENING

RELATED MAJORS: Art; Chinese; Classics; French; German; Japanese; Modern Foreign Language; Podiatry; Psychology; Russian; Spanish

RELATED CAREERS: Art Directors; Art, Drama, and Music Teachers, Postsecondary; Cartoonists; Clinical Psychologists; Counseling Psychologists; Foreign Language and Literature Teachers, Postsecondary; Industrial-Organizational Psychologists; Interpreters and Translators; Multi-Media Artists and Animators; Painters and Illustrators; Podiatrists; Psychology Teachers, Postsecondary; School Psychologists; Sculptors; Sketch Artists

Skill: COMPLEX PROBLEM SOLVING

RELATED MAJORS: Dentistry; Podiatry

RELATED CAREERS: Dentists; Health Specialties Teachers, Postsecondary; Podiatrists

Skill: COORDINATION

RELATED MAJORS: Music; Transportation and Logistics Management

RELATED CAREERS: Administrative Services Managers; Art, Drama, and Music Teachers, Postsecondary; Business Teachers, Postsecondary; Chief Executives; Composers; Logisticians; Music Arrangers and Orchestrators; Music Directors; Storage and Distribution Managers; Transportation Managers

Skill: CRITICAL THINKING

RELATED MAJORS: African-American Studies; American Studies; Area Studies; Law; Medical Technology; Oceanography; Physician Assisting; Women's Studies

© JIST Works

RELATED CAREERS: Administrative Law Judges, Adjudicators, and Hearing Officers; Arbitrators, Mediators, and Conciliators; Area, Ethnic, and Cultural Studies Teachers, Postsecondary; Atmospheric, Earth, Marine, and Space Sciences Teachers, Postsecondary; Biological Science Teachers, Postsecondary; Geologists; Geoscientists, Except Hydrologists and Geographers; Health Specialties Teachers, Postsecondary; Hydrologists; Judges, Magistrate Judges, and Magistrates; Law Clerks; Law Teachers, Postsecondary; Lawyers; Medical and Clinical Laboratory Technologists; Natural Sciences Managers; Physician Assistants

Skill: INSTRUCTING

RELATED MAJORS: Actuarial Science; African-American Studies; American Studies; Animal Science; Area Studies; Art History; Business Education; Chiropractic; Dentistry; Dietetics; Elementary Education; English; Humanities; Orthotics/Prosthetics; Physical Education; Physician Assisting; Political Science; Secondary Education; Sociology; Speech-Language Pathology and Audiology; Veterinary Medicine; Women's Studies

RELATED CAREERS: Actuaries; Animal Scientists; Area, Ethnic, and Cultural Studies Teachers, Postsecondary; Art, Drama, and Music Teachers, Postsecondary; Business Teachers, Postsecondary; Chiropractors; Dentists, General; Dieticians; Education Teachers, Postsecondary; Elementary School Teachers, Except Special Education; English Language and Literature Teachers, Postsecondary; Fitness Trainers and Aerobic Instructors; Health Specialties Teachers, Postsecondary; Medical Appliance Technicians; Orthotists and Prosthetists; Physician Assistants; Political Scientists; Preschool Teachers, Except Special Education; Secondary School Teachers, Except Special and Vocational Education; Sociologists; Sociology Teachers, Postsecondary; Speech-Language Pathologists; Veterinarians

Skill: JUDGMENT AND DECISION MAKING

RELATED MAJORS: Accounting; Criminal Justice/Law Enforcement; Finance; Optometry

RELATED CAREERS: Accountants; Auditors; Bailiffs; Budget Analysts; Business Teachers, Postsecondary; Child Support, Missing Persons, and Unemployment Insurance Fraud Investigators; Credit Analysts; Criminal Investigators and Special Agents; Criminal Justice and Law Enforcement Teachers, Postsecondary; Financial Analysts; Financial Examiners; Financial Managers, Branch or Department; Highway Patrol Pilots; Immigration and Customs Inspectors; Loan Officers; Optometrists; Personal Financial Advisors; Police Detectives; Tax Examiners, Collectors, and Revenue Agents; Treasurers, Controllers, and Chief Financial Officers

(continued)

(continued)

Skill: LEARNING STRATEGIES

RELATED MAJORS: Actuarial Science; Business Education; Chiropractic; Early Childhood Education; Elementary Education; English; Geography; Humanities; Library Science; Occupational Therapy; Orthotics/Prosthetics; Physical Education; Physical Therapy; Secondary Education; Sociology; Special Education; Speech-Language Pathology and Audiology

RELATED CAREERS: Actuaries; Audiologists; Business Teachers, Postsecondary; Chiropractors; Coaches and Scouts; Elementary School Teachers, Except Special Education; English Language and Literature Teachers, Postsecondary; Fitness Trainers and Aerobics Instructors; Geographers; Health Specialties Teachers, Postsecondary; Librarians; Middle School Teachers, Except Special and Vocational Education; Occupational Therapists; Orthotists and Prosthetists; Physical Therapists; Preschool Teachers, Except Special Education; Secondary School Teachers, Except Special and Vocational Education; Sociologists; Sociology Teachers, Postsecondary; Special Education Teachers, Middle School; Special Education Teachers, Preschool, Kindergarten, and Elementary School; Special Education Teachers, Secondary School; Speech-Language Pathologists; Vocational Education Teachers, Secondary School

Skill: MANAGEMENT OF FINANCIAL RESOURCES

RELATED MAJORS: Accounting; Advertising; Agricultural Business and Economics; Architecture; Business Management; Finance; Forestry; Geophysics; Hotel/Motel and Restaurant Management; Industrial Engineering; International Business; International Relations; Library Science; Mechanical Engineering; Parks and Recreation Management; Public Administration; Public Relations; Transportation and Logistics Management; Urban Studies

RELATED CAREERS: Accountants; Administrative Services Managers; Advertising and Promotions Managers; Agricultural Crop Farm Managers; Architects, Except Landscape and Naval; Budget Analysts; Business Teachers, Postsecondary; Chief Executives; Credit Analysts; Emergency Management Specialists; Farmers and Ranchers; Financial Analysts; Financial Managers, Branch or Department; Food Service Managers; Foresters; General and Operations Managers; Geologists; Government Service Executives; Industrial Engineers; Librarians; Loan Officers; Lodging Managers; Logisticians; Mechanical Engineers; Political Scientists; Private Sector Executives; Public Relations Specialists; Recreation Workers; Sociologists; Storage and Distribution Managers; Transportation Managers

Skill: MANAGEMENT OF MATERIAL RESOURCES

RELATED MAJORS: Agricultural Business and Economics; Agronomy and Crop Science; Animal Science; International Business; Operations Management; Public Administration

---

© JIST Works

RELATED CAREERS: Administrative Services Managers; Agricultural Crop Farm Managers; Agricultural Sciences Teachers, Postsecondary; Agricultural Technicians; Animal Scientists, Business Teachers, Postsecondary; Chief Executives; Computer and Information Systems Managers; Construction Managers; Emergency Management Specialists; First-Line Supervisors/Managers of Mechanics, Installers, and Repairers; First-Line Supervisors/Managers of Production and Operating Workers; General and Operations Managers; Government Service Executives; Industrial Production Managers; Logisticians; Postmasters and Mail Superintendents; Private Sector Executives; Storage and Distribution Managers; Transportation Managers

Skill: MANAGEMENT OF PERSONNEL RESOURCES

RELATED MAJORS: Agronomy and Crop Science; Animal Science; Business Management; Drama/Theater Arts; Film/Cinema Studies; Health Information Systems Administration; Hospital/Health Facilities Administration; Hotel/Motel and Restaurant Management; Industrial and Labor Relations; International Business; Marketing; Operations Management; Optometry; Parks and Recreation Management; Public Administration; Transportation and Logistics Management

RELATED CAREERS: Administrative Services Managers; Agricultural Crop Farm Managers; Animal Scientists; Art, Drama, and Music Teachers, Postsecondary; Business Teachers, Postsecondary; Chief Executives; Compensation and Benefits Managers; Construction Managers; Cost Estimators; Directors—Stage, Motion Pictures, Television, and Radio; Emergency Management Specialists; Farmers and Ranchers; Food Service Managers; General and Operations Managers; Government Service Executives; Industrial Production Managers; Lodging Managers; Logisticians; Management Analysts; Marketing Managers; Medical and Health Services Managers; Optometrists; Personnel Recruiters; Postmasters and Mail Superintendents; Private Sector Executives; Producers; Recreation Workers; Sales Managers; Social and Community Service Managers; Storage and Distribution Managers; Transportation Managers

Skill: MATHEMATICS

RELATED MAJORS: Astronomy; Geology; Mathematics; Physics; Statistics

RELATED CAREERS: Astronomers; Atmospheric, Earth, Marine, and Space Sciences Teachers, Postsecondary; Geologists; Geoscientists, Except Hydrologists and Geographers; Hydrologists; Mathematical Science Teachers, Postsecondary; Natural Sciences Managers; Physicists; Physics Teachers, Postsecondary; Statisticians

Skill: NEGOTIATION

RELATED MAJORS: Advertising; Business Management; Economics; Environmental Science; Industrial and Labor Relations; Insurance; Law; Marketing; Wildlife Management

(continued)

(continued)

RELATED CAREERS: Administrative Law Judges, Adjudicators, and Hearing Officers; Administrative Services Managers; Advertising and Promotions Managers; Advertising Sales Agents; Arbitrators, Mediators, and Conciliators; Business Teachers, Postsecondary; Chief Executives; Compensation and Benefits Managers; Construction Managers; Cost Estimators; Economists; Fish and Game Wardens; General and Operations Managers; Insurance Adjusters, Examiners, and Investigators; Insurance Sales Agents; Judges, Magistrate Judges, and Magistrates; Law Clerks; Lawyers; Management Analysts; Marketing Managers; Private Sector Executives; Sales Managers

Skill: OPERATION MONITORING

RELATED MAJORS: Food Science

RELATED CAREERS: Agricultural Sciences Teachers, Postsecondary; Agricultural Technicians; Chemical Technicians; Food Science Technicians; Food Scientists and Technologists

Skill: OPERATIONS ANALYSIS

RELATED MAJORS: Aeronautical/Aerospace Engineering; Agricultural Engineering; Architecture; Bioengineering; Chemical Engineering; Civil Engineering; Electrical Engineering; Graphic Design, Commercial Art and Illustration; Landscape Architecture; Management Information Systems; Materials Science; Mechanical Engineering; Metallurgical Engineering; Petroleum Engineering

RELATED CAREERS: Aerospace Engineers; Agricultural Engineers; Architects, Except Landscape and Naval; Architecture Teachers, Postsecondary; Chemical Engineers; Civil Engineers; Commercial and Industrial Designers; Computer and Information Systems Managers; Computer Programmers; Database Administrators; Electrical Engineers; Electronics Engineers, Except Computer; Engineering Managers; Engineering Teachers, Postsecondary; Graphic Designers; Landscape Architects; Materials Engineers; Materials Scientists; Mechanical Engineers; Multi-Media Artists and Animators; Petroleum Engineers

Skill: PERSUASION

RELATED MAJORS: Advertising; Family and Consumer Sciences; Health Information Systems Administration; Hospital/Health Facilities Administration; Human Resources Management; Industrial and Labor Relations; Industrial Design; Insurance; Interior Design; Law; Library Science; Marketing; Medicine; Political Science; Psychology; Public Relations; Secondary Education; Wildlife Management

RELATED CAREERS: Administrative Law Judges, Adjudicators, and Hearing Officers; Advertising and Promotions Managers; Arbitrators, Mediators, and Conciliators; Clinical Psychologists; Commercial and Industrial Designers; Communications Teachers, Postsecondary; Compensation and Benefits Managers; Counseling

© JIST Works

Psychologists; Family and General Practitioners; Insurance Sales Agents; Interior Designers; Internists, General; Judges, Magistrate Judges, and Magistrates; Lawyers; Librarians; Marketing Managers; Medical and Health Services Managers; Political Science Teachers, Postsecondary; Political Scientists; Public Relations Managers; Sales Representatives, Wholesale and Manufacturing, Except Technical and Scientific Products; Secondary School Teachers, Except Special and Vocational Education; Surgeons; Zoologists and Wildlife Biologists

Skill: PROGRAMMING

RELATED MAJORS: Computer Engineering; Computer Science; Graphic Design, Commercial Art and Illustration; Management Information Systems

RELATED CAREERS: Commercial and Industrial Designers; Computer and Information Systems Managers; Computer Hardware Engineers; Computer Programmers; Computer Science Teachers, Postsecondary; Computer Software Engineers, Applications; Computer Software Engineers, Systems Software; Database Administrators; Engineering Managers; Engineering Teachers, Postsecondary; Graphic Designers; Multi-Media Artists and Animators

Skill: READING COMPREHENSION

RELATED MAJORS: Biochemistry; Communications Studies/Speech; Journalism and Mass Communications; Microbiology; Pharmacy; Soil Science; Veterinary Medicine

RELATED CAREERS: Agricultural Sciences Teachers, Postsecondary; Biochemists; Biological Science Teachers, Postsecondary; Biophysicists; Broadcast News Analysts; Caption Writers; Communications Teachers, Postsecondary; Copy Writers; Creative Writers; Editors; Health Specialties Teachers, Postsecondary; Medical Scientists, Except Epidemiologists; Microbiologists; Natural Sciences Managers; Pharmacists; Poets and Lyricists; Public Address System and Other Announcers; Reporters and Correspondents; Soil Scientists; Veterinarians

Skill: SCIENCE

RELATED MAJORS: Astronomy; Biochemistry; Biology; Botany; Chemistry; Chiropractic; Dentistry; Geology; Geophysics; Microbiology; Occupational Health and Industrial Hygiene; Oceanography; Physics; Podiatry; Soil Science; Veterinary Medicine; Zoology

RELATED CAREERS: Agricultural Sciences Teachers, Postsecondary; Astronomers; Atmospheric, Earth, Marine, and Space Sciences Teachers, Postsecondary; Biochemists; Biological Science Teachers, Postsecondary; Biophysicists; Chemists; Chiropractors; Dentists, General; Geologists; Geoscientists, Except Hydrologists and Geographers; Health Specialties Teachers, Postsecondary; Hydrologists; Medical Scientists, Except Epidemiologists; Microbiologists; Natural Sciences Managers;

(continued)

(continued)

Occupational Health and Safety Specialists; Physicists; Podiatrists; Soil Scientists; Veterinarians; Zoologists and Wildlife Biologists

Skill: Service Orientation

RELATED MAJORS: Criminal Justice/Law Enforcement; Health Information Systems Administration; Hospital/Health Facilities Administration; Human Resources Management; Insurance; Nursing (R.N. Training); Parks and Recreation Management; Philosophy; Public Relations; Religion/Religious Studies; Social Work

RELATED CAREERS: Advertising and Promotions Managers; Child, Family, and School Social Workers; Clergy; Communications Teachers, Postsecondary; Compensation and Benefits Managers; Compensation, Benefits, and Job Analysis Specialists; Directors, Religious Activities and Education; Employment Interviewers, Private or Public Employment Service; Insurance Sales Agents; Marriage and Family Therapists; Medical and Health Services Managers; Nursing Instructors and Teachers, Postsecondary; Personnel Recruiters; Philosophy and Religion Teachers, Postsecondary; Police Patrol Officers; Probation Officers and Correctional Treatment Specialists; Public Relations Managers; Public Relations Specialists; Recreation Workers; Registered Nurses; Training and Development Specialists

Skill: Social Perceptiveness

RELATED MAJORS: Business Education; Criminal Justice/Law Enforcement; Early Childhood Education; Elementary Education; English; Family and Consumer Sciences; Hotel/Motel and Restaurant Management; Human Resources Management; Industrial/Technology Education; Medicine; Nursing (R.N. Training); Philosophy; Psychology; Religion/Religious Studies; Social Work; Special Education

RELATED CAREERS: Business Teachers, Postsecondary; Child, Family, and School Social Workers; Clergy; Clinical Psychologists; Compensation and Benefits Managers; Counseling Psychologists; Elementary School Teachers, Except Special Education; English Language and Literature Teachers, Postsecondary; Family and General Practitioners; Food Service Managers; Industrial-Organizational Psychologists; Internists, General; Lodging Managers; Nursing Instructors and Teachers, Postsecondary; Philosophy and Religion Teachers, Postsecondary; Police Patrol Officers; Preschool Teachers, Except Special Education; Psychology Teachers, Postsecondary; Registered Nurses; Secondary School Teachers, Except Special and Vocational Education; Special Education Teachers, Middle School; Special Education Teachers, Secondary School; Surgeons; Training and Development Specialists; Vocational Education Teachers, Secondary School

© JIST Works

Skill: SPEAKING

RELATED MAJORS: Chinese; Classics; Drama/Theater Arts; Film/Cinema Studies; French; German; Interior Design; Japanese; Modern Foreign Language; Music; Russian; Spanish

RELATED CAREERS: Actors, Art, Drama, and Music Teachers, Postsecondary; Camera Operators, Television, Video, and Motion Picture; Composers; Directors—Stage, Motion Pictures, Television, and Radio; Film and Video Editors; Foreign Language and Literature Teachers, Postsecondary; Interior Designers; Interpreters and Translators; Music Arrangers and Orchestrators; Music Directors; Producers Program Directors; Talent Directors; Technical Directors/Managers

Skill: SYSTEMS EVALUATION

RELATED MAJORS: Finance; International Relations

RELATED CAREERS: Budget Analysts; Business Teachers, Postsecondary; Credit Analysts; Financial Analysts; Financial Managers, Branch or Department; Government Service Executives; Loan Officers; Personal Financial Advisors; Political Science Teachers, Postsecondary; Political Scientists; Treasurers, Controllers, and Chief Financial Officers

Skill: TECHNOLOGY DESIGN

RELATED MAJORS: Aeronautical/Aerospace Engineering; Agricultural Engineering; Architecture; Bioengineering; Chemical Engineering; Chemistry; Civil Engineering; Computer Engineering; Computer Science; Electrical Engineering; Graphic Design, Commercial Art and Illustration; Industrial Engineering; Landscape Architecture; Management Information Systems; Materials Science; Metallurgical Engineering; Petroleum Engineering

RELATED CAREERS: Aerospace Engineers; Agricultural Engineers; Architects, Except Landscape and Naval; Architecture Teachers, Postsecondary; Chemical Engineers; Chemists; Civil Engineers; Commercial and Industrial Designers; Computer and Information Systems Managers; Computer Hardware Engineers; Computer Programmers; Computer Science Teachers, Postsecondary; Computer Software Engineers, Applications; Computer Software Engineers, Systems Software; Database Administrators; Electrical Engineers; Electronics Engineers, Except Computer; Engineering Managers; Engineering Teachers, Postsecondary; Graphic Designers; Industrial Engineers; Landscape Architects; Materials Engineers; Materials Scientists; Petroleum Engineers

(continued)

(continued)

Skill: TIME MANAGEMENT

RELATED MAJORS: Accounting; Agricultural Business and Economics; Film/Cinema Studies; Industrial Design; Journalism and Mass Communications; Nursing (R.N. Training)

RELATED CAREERS: Accountants; Art, Drama, and Music Teachers, Postsecondary; Auditors; Broadcast News Analysts; Budget Analysts; Business Teachers, Postsecondary; Camera Operators, Television, Video, and Motion Picture; Commercial and Industrial Designers; Credit Analysts; Directors—Stage, Motion Pictures, Television, and Radio; Financial Examiners; Film and Video Editors; First-Line Supervisors and Manager/Supervisors—Agricultural Crop Workers; Graphic Designers; Nursing Instructors and Teachers, Postsecondary; Producers; Program Directors; Registered Nurses; Talent Directors; Tax Examiners, Collectors, and Revenue Agents; Technical Directors/Managers

Skill: TROUBLESHOOTING

RELATED MAJORS: Computer Engineering; Computer Science

RELATED CAREERS: Computer and Information Systems Managers; Computer Hardware Engineers; Computer Science Teachers, Postsecondary; Computer Software Engineers, Applications; Computer Software Engineers, Systems Software; Database Administrators; Engineering Managers; Engineering Teachers, Postsecondary

Skill: WRITING

RELATED MAJORS: African-American Studies; American Studies; Anthropology; Archeology; Area Studies; Chinese; Classics; Communications Studies/Speech; Economics; French; Geography; German; History; Humanities; Journalism and Mass Communications; Occupational Health and Industrial Hygiene; Philosophy; Political Science; Sociology; Spanish; Urban Studies; Women's Studies

RELATED CAREERS: Anthropologists; Anthropology and Archeology Teachers, Postsecondary; Archeologists; Area, Ethnic, and Cultural Studies Teachers, Postsecondary; Art, Drama, and Music Teachers, Postsecondary; Communications Teachers, Postsecondary; Economists; Editors; Geographers; Geography Teachers, Postsecondary; Health Specialties Teachers, Postsecondary; History Teachers; Postsecondary; Interpreters and Translators; Market Research Analysts; Occupational Health and Safety Specialists; Philosophy and Religion Teachers, Postsecondary; Political Science Teachers, Postsecondary; Political Scientists; Reporters and Correspondents; Sociologists; Sociology Teachers, Postsecondary; Writers and Authors

© JIST Works

Use the following worksheet to write down the most appealing college majors and careers that correspond with the three skills you marked earlier in this chapter.

COLLEGE MAJORS AND CAREERS THAT RELATE TO MY SKILLS

_____

_____

_____

_____

_____

_____

_____

_____

Key Points: Chapter 3

- Part of a good career decision (which will shape your decision about your major) is matching your skills with a career's demands for skills.

- Your past experiences in school and work can help you understand which skills you are good at and enjoy using.

Chapter 4

What Were Your Favorite High School Courses?

A good way to predict how well people will like college courses is to ask them how much they liked similar high school courses. In addition, most people earn their highest grades in college courses that are similar to the high school courses in which they did well. Your high school experiences can also help to predict your satisfaction and success in various careers. Therefore, this is a good time for you to give some thought to the high school courses that you liked and in which you earned high grades.

My Favorite High School Courses

In the following worksheet, write down the names of three favorite high school courses.

MY FAVORITE HIGH SCHOOL COURSES
1. _____
2. _____
3. _____

Relating High School Courses to College Majors and Careers

Next, with those courses in mind, look over the information in the following table and circle related college majors and careers.

> **Tip:** *Basic courses in some subjects (e.g., math and English) are commonly required for almost everybody who goes to high school. That's why, in the following table, you'll find that these subjects are cross-referenced to high-level courses, such as pre-calculus and literature, that relate more directly to the requirements of specific majors.*

High School Courses and Related College Majors and Careers

High School Course: ART

RELATED MAJORS: Advertising; Architecture; Art; Art History; Graphic Design, Commercial Art, and Illustration; Industrial Design; Interior Design; Landscape Architecture

RELATED CAREERS: Advertising and Promotions Managers; Architects; Architecture Teachers, Postsecondary; Art Directors; Art, Drama, and Music Teachers, Postsecondary; Cartoonists; Commercial and Industrial Designers; Graphic Designers; Interior Designers; Landscape Architects; Medical Appliance Technicians; Multi-Media Artists and Animators; Orthotics/Prosthetics; Painters and Illustrators; Sculptors; Sketch Artists

High School Course: BIOLOGY

RELATED MAJORS: Agricultural Business and Economics; Agronomy and Crop Science; Animal Science; Biochemistry; Bioengineering; Biology; Botany; Chiropractic; Dentistry; Dietetics; Environmental Science; Food Science; Forestry; Medical Technology; Medicine; Microbiology; Nursing (R.N. Training); Optometry; Orthotics/Prosthetics; Parks and Recreation Management; Pharmacy; Physician Assisting; Podiatry; Soil Science; Veterinary Medicine; Wildlife Management; Zoology

RELATED CAREERS: Agricultural Sciences Teachers, Postsecondary; Agricultural Technicians; Anesthesiologists; Biochemists; Biological Science Teachers, Postsecondary; Biophysicists; Chiropractors; Dentists, General; Dieticians and Nutritionists; Environmental Science and Protection Technicians, Including Health; Environmental Science Teachers, Postsecondary; Environmental Scientists and Specialists, Including Health; Family and General Practitioners; First-Line Supervisors and Manager/Supervisors—Animal Care Workers, Except Livestock; Food Scientists and Technologists; Foresters; Internists, General; Medical and Clinical Laboratory Technologists; Medical Scientists, Except Epidemiologists; Micro-biologists; Nursery and Greenhouse Managers; Obstetricians and Gynecologists; Optometrists; Orthotists and Prosthetists; Park Naturalists; Pediatricians, General; Pharmacists; Physician Assistants; Podiatrists; Registered Nurses; Soil Conservationists; Surgeons; Veterinarians; Zoologists and Wildlife Biologists

High School Course: CALCULUS

RELATED MAJORS: Actuarial Science; Aeronautical/Aerospace Engineering; Agricultural Engineering; Architecture; Astronomy; Biochemistry; Bioengineering; Chemical Engineering; Chemistry; Civil Engineering; Computer Engineering; Computer Science; Electrical Engineering; Geology; Geophysics; Mathematics; Mechanical Engineering; Metallurgical Engineering; Petroleum Engineering; Pharmacy; Physics; Statistics

(continued)

(continued)

RELATED CAREERS: Actuaries; Aerospace Engineers; Agricultural Engineers; Architects, Astronomers; Biochemists; Chemical Engineers; Chemists; Civil Engineers; Computer Hardware Engineers; Computer Software Engineers, Applications; Computer Software Engineers, Systems Software; Economists; Electrical Engineers; Electronics Engineers, Except Computer; Engineering Managers; Engineering Teachers, Postsecondary; Geologists, Materials Engineers; Mathematical Science Teachers, Postsecondary; Mathematicians; Mechanical Engineers; Petroleum Engineers; Pharmacists; Physicists; Statisticians

High School Course: CHEMISTRY

RELATED MAJORS: Agronomy and Crop Science; Animal Science; Biochemistry; Bioengineering; Biology; Botany; Chemical Engineering; Chemistry; Chiropractic; Dentistry; Dietetics; Environmental Science; Food Science; Forestry; Geology; Geophysics; Materials Science; Medical Technology; Medicine; Metallurgical Engineering; Microbiology; Nursing (R.N. Training); Oceanography; Pharmacy; Soil Science; Wildlife Management; Zoology

RELATED CAREERS: Agricultural Technicians; Anesthesiologists; Animal Scientists; Atmospheric, Earth, Marine, and Space Sciences Teachers, Postsecondary; Biochemists; Biological Science Teachers, Postsecondary; Biological Technicians; Chemical Engineers; Chemical Technicians; Chemistry Teachers, Postsecondary; Chemists; Chiropractors; Dentists, General; Dieticians and Nutritionists; Environmental Compliance Inspectors; Farmers and Ranchers; Forest and Conservation Workers; Food Scientists and Technologists; Foresters; Geologists; Geoscientists, Except Hydrologists and Geographers; Health Specialties Teachers, Postsecondary; Materials Scientists; Medical and Clinical Laboratory Technologists; Medical Scientists, Except Epidemiologists; Natural Sciences Managers; Pharmacists; Plant Scientists; Registered Nurses; Soil Scientists; Zoologists and Wildlife Biologists

High School Course: CHINESE, *See Foreign Language*

High School Course: COMPUTER SCIENCE

RELATED MAJORS: Accounting; Actuarial Science; Aeronautical/Aerospace Engineering; Agricultural Engineering; Architecture; Astronomy; Bioengineering; Chemical Engineering; Civil Engineering; Computer Engineering; Computer Science; Electrical Engineering; Graphic Design, Commercial Art, and Illustration; Health Information Systems Administration; Industrial Design; Industrial Engineering; Library Science; Management Information Systems; Materials Science; Mathematics; Mechanical Engineering; Metallurgical Engineering; Operations Management; Petroleum Engineering; Physics; Statistics; Transportation and Logistics Management

© JIST Works

RELATED CAREERS: Accountants; Actuaries; Aerospace Engineers; Agricultural Engineers; Architects, Except Landscape and Naval; Auditors; Astronomers; Avionics Technicians; Chemical Engineers; Civil Engineers; Commercial and Industrial Designers; Computer and Information Systems Managers; Computer Hardware Engineers; Computer Operators; Computer Programmers; Computer Science Teachers, Postsecondary; Computer Security Specialists; Computer Software Engineers, Applications; Computer Software Engineers, Systems Software; Computer Systems Analysts; Database Administrators; Data Processing Equipment Repairers; Electrical and Electronic Inspectors and Testers; Electrical Engineers; Electronics Engineers, Except Computer; Engineering Managers; Graphic Designers; Industrial Engineers; Librarians; Logisticians; Materials Engineers; Mathematicians; Mechanical Engineers; Medical and Health Services Managers; Network and Computer Systems Administrators; Network Systems and Data Communications Analysts; Petroleum Engineers; Physicists; Statisticians; Storage and Distribution Managers

High School Course: DANCE

RELATED MAJORS: Dance

RELATED CAREERS: Art, Drama, and Music Teachers, Postsecondary; Choreographers; Dancers; Talent Directors

High School Course: ENGLISH, *See Literature*

High School Course: FOREIGN LANGUAGE

RELATED MAJORS: African-American Studies; American Studies; Anthropology; Archeology; Area Studies; Chinese; Classics; Communications Studies/Speech; Early Childhood Education; Elementary Education; English; Film/Cinema Studies; French; Geography; German; History; Humanities; International Business; International Relations; Japanese; Journalism and Mass Communications; Library Science; Modern Foreign Language; Music; Philosophy; Public Relations; Religion/Religious Studies; Russian; Secondary Education; Social Work; Spanish; Urban Studies

RELATED CAREERS: Anthropologists; Anthropology and Archeology Teachers, Postsecondary; Area, Ethnic, and Cultural Studies Teacher, Postsecondary; Caption Writers; Foreign Language and Literature Teachers, Postsecondary; Geographers; History Teachers, Postsecondary; Interpreters and Translators; Philosophy and Religion Teachers, Postsecondary; Political Scientists; Public Relations Managers

High School Course: FRENCH, *See Foreign Language*

(continued)

(continued)

High School Course: GEOGRAPHY

RELATED MAJORS: Environmental Science; Forestry; Geography; International Business

RELATED CAREERS: Anthropologists; Anthropology and Archeology Teachers, Postsecondary; Atmospheric, Earth, Marine, and Space Sciences Teachers, Postsecondary; Cartographers and Photogrammetrists; Elementary School Teachers, Except Special Education; Environmental Science Teachers, Postsecondary; Environmental Scientists and Specialists; Foreign Language and Literature Teachers, Postsecondary; Foresters; Geographers; Geography Teachers, Postsecondary; Geologists; History Teachers, Postsecondary; Hydrologists; Interpreters and Translators; Surveyors

---

High School Course: GEOMETRY, *See Pre-Calculus or Calculus*

High School Course: GERMAN, *See Foreign Language*

High School Course: HISTORY

RELATED MAJORS: African-American Studies; American Studies; Anthropology; Archeology; Area Studies; Art History; Chinese; Classics; French; Geography; German; History; Humanities; International Relations; Japanese; Law; Modern Foreign Language; Political Science; Religion/Religious Studies; Russian; Spanish; Urban Studies; Women's Studies

RELATED CAREERS: Administrative Law Judges, Adjudicators, and Hearing Officers; Anthropologists; Anthropology and Archeology Teachers, Postsecondary; Archeologists; Area, Ethnic, and Cultural Studies Teachers, Postsecondary; Art, Drama, and Music Teachers, Postsecondary; Clergy; Foreign Language and Literature Teachers, Postsecondary; Geographers; Historians; History Teachers, Postsecondary; Interpreters and Translators; Judges, Magistrate Judges, and Magistrates; Lawyers; Museum Technicians and Conservators; Political Science Teachers, Postsecondary; Political Scientists

---

High School Course: HOME ECONOMICS

RELATED MAJORS: Family and Consumer Sciences

RELATED CAREERS: Animal Scientists; Dietetic Technicians; Dietitians and Nutritionists; Farm and Home Management Advisors; Food Science Technicians; Food Scientists and Technologists; Food Service Managers; Purchasing Agents and Buyers, Farm Products

---

High School Course: INDUSTRIAL ARTS

RELATED MAJORS: Industrial/Technology Education

© JIST Works

RELATED CAREERS: Vocational Education Teachers, Middle School; Vocational Education Teachers, Secondary School

High School Course: JAPANESE, *See Foreign Language*

High School Course: KEYBOARDING

RELATED MAJORS: Business Education; Library Science

RELATED CAREERS: Business Teachers, Postsecondary; Education Teachers, Postsecondary; Librarians; Library Science Teachers, Postsecondary; Vocational Education Teachers, Middle School; Vocational Education Teachers, Postsecondary

High School Course: LITERATURE

RELATED MAJORS: African-American Studies; American Studies; Area Studies; Art; Art History; Chinese; Classics; Drama/Theater Arts; English; Film/Cinema Studies; French; German; Humanities; Japanese; Journalism and Mass Communications; Russian; Spanish; Women's Studies

RELATED CAREERS: Actors; Area, Ethnic, and Cultural Studies Teachers, Postsecondary; Drama, and Music Teachers, Postsecondary; Copy Writers; Directors—Stage, Motion Pictures, Television, and Radio; Editors; English Language and Literature Teachers, Postsecondary; Foreign Language and Literature Teachers, Postsecondary; Interpreters and Translators; Poets and Lyricists; Producers; Reporters and Correspondents

High School Course: MECHANICAL DRAWING

RELATED MAJORS: Graphic Design, Commercial Art, and Illustration; Industrial Design; Industrial/Technology Education

RELATED CAREERS: Commercial and Industrial Designers; Graphic Designers; Multimedia Artists and Animators; Vocational Education Teachers, Middle School; Vocational Education Teachers, Postsecondary; Vocational Education Teachers, Secondary School

High School Course: MUSIC

RELATED MAJORS: Dance; Music

RELATED CAREERS: Art, Drama, and Music Teachers, Postsecondary; Choreographers; Composers; Dancers; Music Arrangers and Orchestrators; Music Directors; Musicians and Singers; Talent Directors

High School Course: OFFICE COMPUTER APPLICATIONS

RELATED MAJORS: Business Education; Health Information Systems Administration; Hospital/Health Facilities Administration; Library Science

(continued)

(continued)

RELATED CAREERS: Business Teachers, Postsecondary; Librarians; Library Science Teachers, Postsecondary; Medical and Health Services Managers; Vocational Education Teachers, Middle School; Vocational Education Teachers, Postsecondary; Vocational Education Teachers, Secondary School

High School Course: PHOTOGRAPHY

RELATED MAJORS: Film/Cinema Studies; Graphic Design, Commercial Art, and Illustration; Industrial Design

RELATED CAREERS: Camera Operators, Television, Video, and Motion Picture; Film and Video Editors; Graphic Designers; Industrial Designers; Multi-Media Artists and Animators; Photographers

High School Course: PHYSICS/PRINCIPLES OF TECHNOLOGY

RELATED MAJORS: Aeronautical/Aerospace Engineering; Architecture; Astronomy; Bioengineering; Chemical Engineering; Chemistry; Chiropractic; Civil Engineering; Computer Engineering; Computer Science; Dentistry; Electrical Engineering; Geology; Geophysics; Materials Science; Mechanical Engineering; Medicine; Metallurgical Engineering; Oceanography; Optometry; Orthotics/Prosthetics; Petroleum Engineering; Physics; Podiatry; Speech-Language Pathology and Audiology; Veterinary Medicine

RELATED CAREERS: Aerospace Engineers; Agricultural Engineers; Anesthesiologists; Architects, Except Landscape and Naval; Astronomers; Atmospheric, Earth, Marine, and Space Sciences Teachers, Postsecondary; Audiologists; Chemical Engineers; Chemists; Chiropractors; Civil Engineers; Computer and Information Systems Managers; Computer Hardware Engineers; Computer Science Teachers, Postsecondary; Computer Software Engineers, Applications; Computer Software Engineers, Systems Software; Dentists; Electrical Engineers; Electronics Engineers, Except Computer; Engineering Managers; Engineering Teachers, Postsecondary; Family and General Practitioners; Geologists; Health Specialties Teachers, Postsecondary; Hydrologists; Internists, General; Materials Engineers; Mechanical Engineers; Natural Sciences Managers; Optometrists; Orthotists and Prosthetists; Petroleum Engineers; Physicists; Physics Teachers, Postsecondary; Podiatrists; Speech-Language Pathologists; Surgeons; Veterinarians

High School Course: PRE-CALCULUS

RELATED MAJORS: Actuarial Science; Aeronautical/Aerospace Engineering; Agricultural Engineering; Astronomy; Bioengineering; Chemical Engineering; Chemistry; Civil Engineering; Computer Engineering; Computer Science; Economics; Electrical Engineering; Geology; Geophysics; Industrial Engineering; Materials Science; Mathematics; Mechanical Engineering; Metallurgical Engineering; Oceanography; Operations Management; Optometry; Petroleum Engineering; Physics; Statistics

© JIST Works

RELATED CAREERS: Actuaries; Aerospace Engineers; Agricultural Engineers; Astronomers; Biomedical Engineers; Chemical Engineers; Chemists; Civil Engineers; Computer Hardware Engineers; Computer Software Engineers, Applications; Computer Software Engineers, Systems Software; Economists; Electrical Engineers; Electronics Engineers, Except Computer; Engineering Managers; Engineering Teachers, Postsecondary; Geologists; Industrial Engineers; Materials Engineers; Mathematical Science Teachers, Postsecondary; Mathematicians; Mechanical Engineers; Operations Research Analysts; Optometrists; Petroleum Engineers; Physicists; Physics Teachers, Postsecondary; Statisticians

High School Course: PUBLIC SPEAKING

RELATED MAJORS: Advertising; African-American Studies; American Studies; Anthropology; Archeology; Business Education; Communications Studies/Speech; Drama/Theater Arts; Early Childhood Education; Elementary Education; Family and Consumer Sciences; French; German; Japanese; Journalism and Mass Communications; Law; Modern Foreign Language; Religion/Religious Studies; Recreation Management; Russian; Secondary Education; Spanish; Special Education; Speech-Language Pathology and Audiology; Women's Studies

RELATED CAREERS: Actors; Administrative Law Judges, Adjudicators, and Hearing Officers; Advertising Sales Agents; Anthropologists; Arbitrators, Mediators, and Conciliators; Archeologists; Area, Ethnic, and Cultural Studies Teachers, Postsecondary; Broadcast News Analysts; Business Teachers, Postsecondary; Clergy; Communications Teachers, Postsecondary; Education Teachers, Postsecondary; Graduate Teaching Assistants; Health Specialties Teachers, Postsecondary; Home Economics Teachers, Postsecondary; Interpreters and Translators; Judges, Magistrate Judges, and Magistrates; Kindergarten Teachers, Except Special Education; Lawyers; Library Science Teachers, Postsecondary; Middle School Teachers, Except Special and Vocational Education; Preschool Teachers, Except Special Education; Public Address System and Other Announcers; Recreation Workers; Reporters and Correspondents; Secondary School Teachers, Except Special and Vocational Education; Special Education Teachers, Middle School; Special Education Teachers, Preschool, Kindergarten, and Elementary School; Special Education Teachers, Secondary School; Speech-Language Pathologists; Telemarketers; Vocational Education Teachers, Middle School; Vocational Education Teachers, Postsecondary; Vocational Education Teachers, Secondary School

High School Course: SOCIAL SCIENCE

RELATED MAJORS: Advertising; African-American Studies; American Studies; Anthropology; Archeology; Area Studies; Art History; Communications Studies/Speech; Criminal Justice/Law Enforcement; Dietetics; Economics; Geography; History; Industrial and Labor Relations; International Relations; Law; Parks and Recreation Management; Political Science; Psychology; Religion/Religious Studies; Social Work; Sociology; Spanish; Urban Studies; Women's Studies

(continued)

(continued)

> **RELATED CAREERS:** Administrative Law Judges, Adjudicators, and Hearing Officers; Advertising Sales Agents; Anthropologists; Anthropology and Archeology Teachers, Postsecondary; Arbitrators, Mediators, and Conciliators; Area, Ethnic, and Cultural Studies Teachers, Postsecondary; Child, Family, and School Social Workers; Child Support, Missing Persons, and Unemployment Insurance Fraud Investigators; Clergy; Clinical Psychologists; Communications Teachers, Postsecondary; Counseling Psychologists; Criminal Investigators and Special Agents; Criminal Justice and Law Enforcement Teachers, Postsecondary; Dieticians and Nutritionists; Economists; Fish and Game Wardens; Geographers; Historians; History Teachers, Postsecondary; Immigration and Customs Inspectors; Industrial-Organizational Psychologists; Judges, Magistrate Judges, and Magistrates; Law Teachers, Postsecondary; Lawyers; Marriage and Family Therapists; Personnel Recruiters; Police Identification and Records Officers; Political Scientists; Probation Officers and Correctional Treatment Specialists; Recreation Workers; Reporters and Correspondents; Social Work Teachers, Postsecondary; Sociologists; Sociology Teachers, Postsecondary
>
> **High School Course:** SPANISH, *See Foreign Language*
>
> **High School Course:** TRIGONOMETRY, *See Pre-Calculus or Calculus*

Find the items in the table that best fit with the three favorite high school courses you listed at the beginning of this chapter. If a lot of majors or careers are listed, try to find some that are linked to more than one of your favorite courses or that otherwise are interesting to you. Then write these college majors and careers in the following worksheet.

COLLEGE MAJORS AND CAREERS THAT RELATE TO MY FAVORITE HIGH SCHOOL COURSES

_____

_____

_____

_____

_____

_____

_____

© JIST Works

Key Points: Chapter 4

- Success in a high school course can predict success in a similar college course and therefore in a related college major.

- Your satisfaction with high school courses can also suggest satisfying careers.

© JIST Works

Chapter 5

Your Hot List of College Majors and Careers

Now that you've done the exercises in the three preceding chapters, it's time for you to assemble a Hot List of College Majors and Careers that deserve your active consideration in chapter 6.

At the end of each of the three exercises in the preceding chapters—concerning interests, skills, and high school courses—you filled out a worksheet with a list of the college majors and careers that were most strongly suggested by each exercise. Look these over now and decide which of the following statements best characterizes what you see:

- **Certain majors and careers appear in the results from all three exercises.** If this is what you find, congratulations! These majors and careers obviously correspond well to your personality, and you should write them in your Hot List on the next page.

- **Certain majors and careers appear in your results from two of the exercises, but none appears in three.** This is still a meaningful finding; these majors and careers probably belong on your Hot List. If many majors and careers fit this description, you might ask yourself whether you feel more confident about one kind of exercise than another. For example, do you feel you have a clearer notion of your interests and favorite high school courses than of your skills? In that case, you might want to give greater weight to the majors and careers that are shared by the results of the exercises relating to your interests and favorite high school courses.

- **There's no pattern at all—no majors or careers appear in the results from more than one of the exercises.** In this case, you need to decide which exercise you trust the most. Different people have different styles of thinking about themselves; for example, some have a much keener awareness of their interests than their skills. Or perhaps the terms used in one exercise seem easier to understand than the terms in the others. Go with the results of the exercise that you feel most confident about. Write those majors and careers in your Hot List.

- **One of the preceding three statements applies to you, but you have a *very* large number of majors on your Hot List.** Here's where the careers can help you—they can help you narrow down the majors you're considering. Find the career that appears most often in the results of the exercises for skills and high school courses. (If no career appears more than once, pick one that seems especially interesting to you.) Then go back to the interest exercise in chapter 2 and find the one-, two-, or three-letter interest code for this career. Identify majors that have this same interest code or a code similar to it. These are strong candidates for your Hot List.

After you have filled in your Hot List and have started investigating the listed majors in chapter 6, you can also use the Hot List as an informal way of recording your impressions:

- If a major appeals to you when you read about it, put a few stars next to the name on the Hot List. The stars can serve to remind you which majors are the hottest of the hot!

- One of the important facts you'll read about the major is what careers it is linked to. When you see a career that looks interesting to you, write its name next to the name of the major on the Hot List (if it's not there already). Later you can use other resources to investigate these jobs in greater detail.

MY HOT LIST OF COLLEGE MAJORS AND CAREERS

_____

_____

_____

_____

_____

_____

_____

_____

(continued)

(continued)

Key Points: Chapter 5

- If a major or career appeals to you for multiple reasons (for example, because of both your interests and your skills), it deserves further exploration and consideration.

- If the exercises in the preceding chapters did not produce consistently "hot" majors or careers, focus on the results of the one or two exercises that you felt most confident doing.

© JIST Works

Chapter 6

Review College Majors and Related Careers

In this chapter, you can get the facts about 120 college majors and the careers related to them. You may learn new things about majors that you thought you knew all about. You may also encounter majors that you never heard of before, or that you don't know well.

The Hot List you created in chapter 5 can help you choose majors to explore here. It may also suggest careers that you can look up in the index to identify related majors in this chapter. But even if you just browse this chapter at random, the facts are organized in a way that makes it easy for you to get an understanding of the major and related careers.

Here's what you'll find for each major:

- **Title, Definition, and CIP Code:** The title is a name that is frequently used for the major, although some majors may also be known under other names. The brief definition is derived from the Classification of Instructional Programs (CIP), a system developed by the U.S. Department of Education to catalog every major. The code number(s) of the related CIP program(s) completes this section.

- **Specializations in the Major:** Most majors allow students to select a "concentration," a "track," or some other way of specializing in one aspect of the field. This list identifies some but may not be exhaustive.

- **Typical Sequence of College Courses:** This section shows a list of courses often required for this major, ordered in a way they might logically be taken. Of course, each college varies on what specific courses they require, what courses they offer, and what sequences they allow. Also, students usually have some freedom to tailor the course content and sequence to their interests and needs.

- **Typical Sequence of High School Courses:** These are high school courses that are considered good preparation for the major. High schools vary on their requirements and offerings, and colleges vary on what courses they prefer as prerequisites.

- **Career Snapshot:** This briefly describes what careers are related to the major. Outlook information that appears here is based on the Department of Labor's *Occupational Outlook Handbook.*

- **Related Job(s):** Here you can see specific facts about the jobs related to the major. The facts are derived from the U.S. Department of Labor and reflect the national average for all workers in the occupation. To help you make sense of the figures, you should know that the average income for all the occupations in this book is about $56,000 and the average rate of growth is 16.2%. (Compare that to the averages of $29,070 income and –5.4% growth for all wage-earning occupations in the economy, and you can see that a college education is a good investment!) Job growth is through 2014. Job openings are annual figures.

- **Characteristics of the Related Jobs:** This section shows the interest type(s) and the most significant skills, values, and work conditions for the related jobs.

Accounting

Prepares individuals to practice the profession of accounting and to perform related business functions. **Related CIP Program:** 52.0301 Accounting.

Specializations in the Major: Accounting computer systems, auditing, cost accounting, financial reporting, forensic accounting, taxation.

Typical Sequence of College Courses: English composition, business writing, introduction to principles of microeconomics, principles of macroeconomics, calculus for business and social sciences, statistics for business and social sciences, introduction to management information systems, introduction to accounting, legal environment of business, principles of management and organization, operations management, strategic management, business finance, introduction to marketing, cost accounting, auditing, taxation of individuals, taxation of corporations, partnerships and estates.

Typical Sequence of High School Courses: English, algebra, geometry, trigonometry, science, foreign language, computer science.

Career Snapshot: Accountants maintain the financial records of an organization and supervise the recording of transactions. They provide information about the fiscal condition and trends of the organization, and figures for tax forms and financial reports. They advise management and, therefore, need good communication skills. A bachelor's degree is sufficient preparation for many entry-level jobs, but some employers prefer a master's degree. Accountants with diverse skills may advance to management after a few years. The job outlook is generally good.

Related Jobs			
Job Title	Average Earnings	Job Growth	Job Openings
1. Accountants	$51,310	22.4%	157,000
2. Auditors	$51,310	22.4%	157,000
3. Budget Analysts	$57,190	13.5%	6,000
4. Business Teachers, Postsecondary	$58,230	32.2%	329,000
5. Credit Analysts	$48,800	3.6%	3,000
6. Financial Examiners	$60,470	9.5%	3,000
7. Tax Examiners, Collectors, and Revenue Agents	$44,000	5.1%	4,000

Jobs 1 and 2 and share 157,000 job openings. Job 4 shares 329,000 job openings with 35 jobs not included in the list.

Characteristics of the Related Jobs: Interests—Conventional; Enterprising; Investigative. **Skills**—Management of financial resources; time management; judgment and decision making; negotiation; mathematics. **Values**—Working conditions; compensation; authority; advancement; responsibility. **Work Conditions**—Sitting; indoors, environmentally controlled; spend time making repetitive motions.

Actuarial Science

Focuses on the mathematical and statistical analysis of risk, and their applications to insurance and other business management problems. **Related CIP Program:** 52.1304 Actuarial Science.

Specializations in the Major: Insurance, investment.

Typical Sequence of College Courses: Calculus, linear algebra, advanced calculus, introduction to computer science, introduction to probability, introduction to actuarial mathematics, mathematical statistics, applied regression, actuarial models, introduction to accounting, principles of microeconomics, principles of macroeconomics, financial management, programming in C, investment analysis, price theory, income and employment theory. **Typical Sequence of High School Courses:** English, algebra, geometry, trigonometry, science, pre-calculus, calculus, computer science.

Career Snapshot: Actuarial science is the analysis of mathematical data to predict the likelihood of certain events, such as death, accident, or disability. Insurance companies are the main employers of actuaries; actuaries determine how much the insurers charge for policies. The usual entry route is a bachelor's degree, but actuaries continue to study and sit for exams to upgrade their professional standing over the course of 5 to 10 years. The occupation is expected to grow at a good pace, and there will probably be many openings for those who are able to pass the series of exams.

Related Jobs			
Job Title	Average Earnings	Job Growth	Job Openings
1. Actuaries	$78,810	23.2%	3,000
2. Business Teachers, Postsecondary	$58,230	32.2%	329,000

Job 2 shares 329,000 job openings with 35 jobs not included in the list.

Characteristics of the Related Jobs: Interests—Conventional; Investigative; Realistic. **Skills**—Instructing; learning strategies; active learning; monitoring; time management. **Values**—Autonomy; working conditions; advancement; recognition; independence. **Work Conditions**—Indoors, environmentally controlled; sitting.

Advertising

Focuses on the creation, execution, transmission, and evaluation of commercial messages in various media intended to promote and sell products, services, and brands; and that prepares individuals to function as advertising assistants, technicians, and managers. **Related CIP Program:** 09.0903 Advertising.

Specializations in the Major: Creative process, management.

© JIST Works

Typical Sequence of College Courses: English composition, oral communication, statistics for business and social sciences, introduction to marketing, introduction to advertising, communications theory, advertising message strategy, communication ethics, advertising media, advertising copy and layout, advertising account planning and research, advertising campaign management, mass communication law, introduction to communication research. **Typical Sequence of High School Courses:** English, algebra, foreign language, art, literature, public speaking, social science.

Career Snapshot: Advertising is a combination of writing, art, and business. Graduates with a bachelor's degree in advertising often go on to jobs in advertising agencies, mostly in large cities. They may start as copywriters and advance to management. Competition can be keen because the industry is considered glamorous. A knowledge of how to advertise on the Internet can be an advantage.

Related Jobs			
Job Title	Average Earnings	Job Growth	Job Openings
1. Advertising and Promotions Managers	$66,560	20.3%	9,000
2. Advertising Sales Agents	$41,410	16.3%	24,000
3. Communications Teachers, Postsecondary	$50,610	32.2%	329,000

Job 3 shares 329,000 job openings with 35 jobs not included in the list.

Characteristics of the Related Jobs: Interests—Enterprising; Artistic; Social. **Skills**—Negotiation; persuasion; management of financial resources; service orientation; social perceptiveness. **Values**—Creativity; working conditions; variety; ability utilization; achievement. **Work Conditions**—Sitting; walking and running.

Aeronautical/Aerospace Engineering

Prepares individuals to apply mathematical and scientific principles to the design, development, and operational evaluation of aircraft, space vehicles, and their systems; applied research on flight characteristics; and the development of systems and procedures for the launching, guidance, and control of air and space vehicles. **Related CIP Program:** 14.0201 Aerospace, Aeronautical, and Astronautical Engineering.

Specializations in the Major: Airframes and aerodynamics, propulsion, spacecraft, testing.

Typical Sequence of College Courses: English composition, technical writing, calculus, differential equations, introduction to computer science, general chemistry, general physics, thermodynamics, introduction to electric circuits, introduction to aerospace engineering, statics, dynamics, materials engineering, fluid mechanics, aircraft systems and propulsion, flight control systems, aerodynamics, aircraft structural design, aircraft stability and control, experimental aerodynamics, senior design project. **Typical Sequence of High School Courses:** English, algebra, geometry, trigonometry, pre-calculus, calculus, chemistry, physics, computer science.

Career Snapshot: Engineers apply scientific principles to real-world problems, finding the optimal solution that balances elegant technology with realistic cost. Aeronautical/aerospace engineers need to learn the specific principles of air flow and resistance, and the workings of various kinds of propulsion systems. Most enter the job market with a bachelor's degree. Some later move into managerial positions. Job outlook is good because for many years other engineering fields were perceived as having a better outlook. Best opportunities are expected in jobs related to defense as opposed to commercial aviation.

Related Jobs			
Job Title	**Average Earnings**	**Job Growth**	**Job Openings**
1. Aerospace Engineers	$82,370	8.3%	6,000
2. Engineering Managers	$99,000	13.0%	15,000
3. Engineering Teachers, Postsecondary	$74,840	32.2%	329,000
Job 3 shares 329,000 job openings with 35 jobs not included in the list.			

Characteristics of the Related Jobs: Interests—Investigative; Realistic; Enterprising. **Skills**—Science; technology design; operations analysis; management of financial resources; persuasion. **Values**—Authority; creativity; autonomy; ability utilization; social status. **Work Conditions**—Sitting; noise levels are distracting or uncomfortable; common protective or safety equipment; indoors, environmentally controlled; high places.

© JIST Works

African-American Studies

Focuses on the history, sociology, politics, culture, and economics of the North American peoples descended from the African diaspora; focusing on the United States, Canada, and the Caribbean, but also including reference to Latin American elements of the diaspora. **Related CIP Program:** 05.0201 African-American/Black Studies.

Specializations in the Major: Behavioral and social inquiry, history and culture, literature, language, and the arts.

Typical Sequence of College Courses: English composition, foreign language, American history, introduction to African American studies, African American literature, African American history, African Diaspora studies, research methods in African American studies, seminar (reporting on research). **Typical Sequence of High School Courses:** English, algebra, foreign language, history, literature, public speaking, social science.

Career Snapshot: African-American studies draws on a number of disciplines, including history, sociology, literature, linguistics, and political science. Usually you can shape the program to emphasize whichever appeals most to you. Graduates frequently pursue higher degrees as a means of establishing a career in a field such as college teaching or the law.

Related Job			
Job Title	*Average Earnings*	*Job Growth*	*Job Openings*
Area, Ethnic, and Cultural Studies Teachers, Postsecondary	$55,660	32.2%	329,000
This job shares 329,000 job openings with 35 jobs not included in the list.			

Characteristics of the Related Job: Interests—Social; Investigative; Artistic. **Skills**—Writing; instructing; critical thinking; persuasion; active learning. **Values**—Authority; social service; creativity; achievement; social status. **Work Conditions**—Sitting; indoors, environmentally controlled.

Agricultural Business and Economics

Focuses on modern business and economic principles involved in the organization, operation, and management of agricultural enterprises.

Related CIP Programs: 01.0101 Agricultural Business and Management, General; 01.0105 Agricultural/Farm Supplies Retailing and Wholesaling; 01.0104 Farm/Farm and Ranch Management.

Specializations in the Major: Agricultural economics, agricultural finance, agricultural marketing and sales, computer applications and data management, farm business management, natural resources management, public policy, ranch business management.

Typical Sequence of College Courses: English composition, oral communication, business math, general biology, introduction to economics, introduction to accounting, introduction to agricultural economics and business, farm/ranch management, computer applications in agriculture, legal and social environment of agriculture, statistics for business and social sciences, microeconomic theory, macroeconomic theory, natural resource economics, agribusiness financial management, introduction to marketing, marketing and pricing agricultural products, technical writing, agricultural policy, quantitative methods in agricultural business. **Typical Sequence of High School Courses:** English, algebra, geometry, trigonometry, biology, chemistry, computer science.

Career Snapshot: Agriculture is a major business in the United States, and graduates of agricultural business and economics programs often work far away from a farm or ranch. They may be employed by a bank that lends to farmers, by a food company that purchases large amounts of agricultural products, by a government agency that sets agricultural policies, or by a manufacturer that sells agricultural equipment, chemicals, or seed. They need to know how agricultural products are produced and how the markets for these products (increasingly global) behave. A bachelor's degree is a common entry route, although a graduate degree is useful for teaching or research positions.

Related Jobs			
Job Title	Average Earnings	Job Growth	Job Openings
1. Agricultural Crop Farm Managers	$50,720	4.0%	20,000
2. Agricultural Sciences Teachers, Postsecondary	$70,610	32.2%	329,000
3. Farm and Home Management Advisors	$41,270	7.7%	2,000

© JIST Works

4. Farmers and Ranchers	$38,600	−14.5%	96,000
5. First-Line Supervisors and Manager/ Supervisors—Agricultural Crop Workers	$36,040	3.6%	11,000
6. First-Line Supervisors and Manager/ Supervisors—Logging Workers	$36,040	3.6%	11,000
7. Fish Hatchery Managers	$50,720	4.0%	20,000
8. Graders and Sorters, Agricultural Products	$16,730	7.9%	4,000
9. Nonfarm Animal Caretakers	$17,640	25.6%	31,000
10. Nursery and Greenhouse Managers	$50,720	4.0%	20,000

Jobs 1, 7, and 10 share 20,000 job openings. Job 2 shares 329,000 job openings with 35 jobs not included in the list. Jobs 5 and 6 share 11,000 job openings.

Characteristics of the Related Jobs: Interest—Realistic. **Skills**— Management of material resources; time management; management of financial resources; persuasion; social perceptiveness. **Values**— Independence; responsibility; autonomy; authority. **Work Conditions**— Outdoors, exposed to weather; contaminants; very hot or cold; minor burns, cuts, bites, or stings; standing.

Agricultural Engineering

Prepares individuals to apply mathematical and scientific principles to the design, development, and operational evaluation of systems, equipment, and facilities used to produce, process, and store agricultural products; to improve the productivity of agricultural methods; and to develop improved agricultural biological systems. **Related CIP Program:** 14.0301 Agricultural/Biological Engineering and Bioengineering.

Specializations in the Major: Agricultural machinery, agricultural structures, environmental engineering, food and fiber processing, irrigation.

Typical Sequence of College Courses: English composition, technical writing, calculus, differential equations, general biology, introduction to computer science, general chemistry, general physics, statics, dynamics, introduction to electric circuits, thermodynamics, numerical analysis, introduction to agricultural engineering, engineering properties of biological materials, fluid mechanics, microcomputer applications, materials engineering, soil and water engineering, agricultural power and machines, biological materials processing, senior design project. **Typical Sequence of High School Courses:** English, algebra, geometry, trigonometry, pre-calculus, biology, calculus, chemistry, computer science.

Career Snapshot: Agricultural engineers use scientific knowledge to solve problems of growing food and fiber crops, building and maintaining agricultural equipment and structures, and processing agricultural products. A bachelor's degree is usually sufficient preparation to enter this field. Often an engineering job can be a springboard for a managerial position. Job outlook is much better than for most other engineering fields, especially in specializations related to biological engineering and environmental protection.

	Related Jobs		
Job Title	**Average Earnings**	**Job Growth**	**Job Openings**
1. Agricultural Engineers	$60,340	12.0%	fewer than 500
2. Engineering Managers	$99,000	13.0%	15,000
3. Engineering Teachers, Postsecondary	$74,840	32.2%	329,000
Job 3 shares 329,000 job openings with 35 jobs not included in the list.			

Characteristics of the Related Jobs: Interests—Enterprising; Investigative; Realistic. **Skills**—Technology design; science; operations analysis; management of financial resources; installation. **Values**—Authority; creativity; autonomy; compensation; ability utilization. **Work Conditions**—Common protective or safety equipment; noise levels are distracting or uncomfortable; hazardous equipment; extremely bright or inadequate lighting; sitting.

Agronomy and Crop Science

Focuses on the chemical, physical, and biological relationships of crops and the soils nurturing them. **Related CIP Program:** 01.1102 Agronomy and Crop Science.

Specializations in the Major: Agro-industry, soil and crop management, turfgrass management.

© JIST Works

Typical Sequence of College Courses: English composition, college algebra, general biology, general chemistry, organic chemistry, genetics, introduction to agricultural economics and business, introduction to soil science, botany, computer applications in agriculture, plant pathology, seed production, crop production, soil fertility, plant nutrition and fertilizers, plant breeding, general entomology, weed control. **Typical Sequence of High School Courses:** Biology, chemistry, algebra, geometry, trigonometry, computer science, English, public speaking.

Career Snapshot: Agronomists and crop scientists look for ways to improve the production and quality of food, feed, and fiber crops. They need to understand the chemical requirements of soils and growing plants and the genetic basis of plant development—especially now that genetic engineering is growing in importance. Those with a bachelor's degree may work in applied research, in managerial jobs in businesses that market to farmers and ranchers, or as agricultural products inspectors. A graduate degree is useful to do basic research and necessary for college teaching. Because agriculture is a vital U.S. industry supported by agricultural extension programs, a large number of agronomists and crop scientists work for federal, state, and local governments, many of them with bachelor's degrees.

Related Jobs			
Job Title	Average Earnings	Job Growth	Job Openings
1. Agricultural Crop Farm Managers	$50,720	4.0%	20,000
2. Agricultural Sciences Teachers, Postsecondary	$70,610	32.2%	329,000
3. Farmers and Ranchers	$38,600	−14.5%	96,000
4. First-Line Supervisors and Manager/ Supervisors—Agricultural Crop Workers	$36,040	3.6%	11,000
5. Plant Scientists	$53,240	13.9%	1,000

Job 1 shares 20,000 job openings with 2 jobs not included in the list. Job 2 shares 329,000 job openings with 35 jobs not included in the list. Job 4 shares 11,000 job openings with 5 jobs not included in the list.

Characteristics of the Related Jobs: Interests—Realistic; Enterprising; Investigative. **Skills**—Science; management of material resources;

management of personnel resources; instructing; writing. **Values**— Authority; autonomy; responsibility; creativity; variety. **Work Conditions**— Outdoors, exposed to weather; hazardous conditions; very hot or cold; contaminants; common protective or safety equipment.

American Studies

Focuses on the history, society, politics, culture, and economics of the United States and its Pre-Columbian and colonial predecessors, including the flow of immigrants from other societies. **Related CIP Program:** 05.0102 American/United States Studies/Civilization.

Specializations in the Major: History and political science, literature, language and the arts, popular culture.

Typical Sequence of College Courses: English composition, American history, American government, American literature, American popular culture, seminar (reporting on research). **Typical Sequence of High School Courses:** English, algebra, foreign language, history, literature, public speaking, social science.

Career Snapshot: American studies is an interdisciplinary major that allows you to concentrate on the aspect of American culture that is of greatest interest to you—for example, history, the arts, or social and ethnic groups. Many, perhaps most, graduates use this major as a springboard to postgraduate or professional training that prepares for a career in college teaching, business, law, the arts, politics, or some other field.

Related Job			
Job Title	Average Earnings	Job Growth	Job Openings
Area, Ethnic, and Cultural Studies Teachers, Postsecondary	$55,660	32.2%	329,000

This job shares 329,000 job openings with 35 jobs not included in the list.

Characteristics of the Related Job: Interests—Social; Investigative; Artistic. **Skills**—Writing; instructing; critical thinking; persuasion; active learning. **Values**—Authority; social service; creativity; achievement; social status. **Work Conditions**—Sitting; indoors, environmentally controlled.

© JIST Works

Animal Science

Focuses on the scientific principles that underlie the breeding and husbandry of agricultural animals, and the production, processing, and distribution of agricultural animal products. **Related CIP Programs:** 01.0902 Agricultural Animal Breeding; 01.0903 Animal Health; 01.0904 Animal Nutrition; 01.0901 Animal Sciences, General; 01.0905 Dairy Science; 01.0906 Livestock Management; 01.0907 Poultry Science.

Specializations in the Major: Production, veterinary research.

Typical Sequence of College Courses: English composition, college algebra, statistics, general biology, general chemistry, organic chemistry, genetics, introduction to agricultural economics and business, introduction to animal science, meats and other animal products, plant physiology, anatomy and physiology of farm animals, animal nutrition and nutritional diseases, feeds and feeding, reproduction of farm animals, animal breeding, marking and grading of livestock and meats. **Typical Sequence of High School Courses:** Biology, chemistry, algebra, geometry, trigonometry, computer science, English, public speaking.

Career Snapshot: Animal science graduates may work directly for farms and ranches that raise animals, or they may work in research, marketing, or sales for pharmaceutical or feed companies that supply farmers, ranchers, and veterinarians. About one-third go on to veterinary school, medical school, or another post-graduate scientific field.

Related Jobs			
Job Title	*Average Earnings*	*Job Growth*	*Job Openings*
1. Agricultural Crop Farm Managers	$50,720	4.0%	20,000
2. Agricultural Sciences Teachers, Postsecondary	$70,610	32.2%	329,000
3. Agricultural Technicians	$30,630	13.4%	1,000
4. Animal Scientists	$43,170	12.9%	fewer than 500
5. Farm and Home Management Advisors	$41,270	7.7%	2,000
6. Farmers and Ranchers	$38,600	–14.5%	96,000

(continued)

(continued)

Job Title	Average Earnings	Job Growth	Job Openings
7. First-Line Supervisors and Manager/Supervisors—Animal Care Workers, Except Livestock	$36,040	3.6%	11,000
8. First-Line Supervisors and Manager/Supervisors—Animal Husbandry Workers	$36,040	3.6%	11,000
9. Food Science Technicians	$30,630	13.4%	1,000

Job 1 shares 20,000 job openings with 2 jobs not included in the list. Job 2 shares 329,000 job openings with 35 jobs not included in the list. Jobs 3 and 9 share 1,000 job openings. Jobs 7 and 8 share 11,000 job openings with each other and with 4 jobs not included in the list.

Characteristics of the Related Jobs: Interests—Realistic; Enterprising; Investigative. **Skills**—Management of personnel resources; instructing; management of material resources; science; time management. **Values**—Authority; autonomy; creativity; responsibility; variety. **Work Conditions**—Outdoors, exposed to weather; hazardous conditions; very hot or cold; contaminants; common protective or safety equipment.

Anthropology

Focuses on the systematic study of human beings, their antecedents and related primates, and their cultural behavior and institutions, in comparative perspective. **Related CIP Program:** 45.0201 Anthropology.

Specializations in the Major: Archaeology, biological/forensic, cultural.

Typical Sequence of College Courses: English composition, general biology, statistics for business and social sciences, human growth and development, introduction to sociology, foreign language, cultural anthropology, physical anthropology, introduction to archeology, language and culture, history of anthropological theory, research methods in anthropology, current issues in anthropology. **Typical Sequence of High School Courses:** Algebra, English, foreign language, social science, history, biology, public speaking, chemistry.

© JIST Works

Career Snapshot: Some anthropologists study the social and cultural behavior of people. They investigate communities throughout the world, focusing on their arts, religions, and economic and social institutions. A graduate degree is usually needed to do research or college teaching in this field, but some graduates with bachelor's degrees find their skills useful in business, such as in marketing research. Other anthropologists specialize in human physical characteristics and may study human remains to understand history or evolution, or to provide evidence in criminal investigations. A graduate degree is usually required for this specialization.

Related Jobs			
Job Title	Average Earnings	Job Growth	Job Openings
1. Anthropologists	$44,620	17.0%	fewer than 500
2. Anthropology and Archeology Teachers, Postsecondary	$60,190	32.2%	329,000

Job 2 shares 329,000 job openings with 35 jobs not included in the list.

Characteristics of the Related Jobs: Interests—Investigative; Social; Artistic. **Skills**—Writing; science; active learning; critical thinking; reading comprehension. **Values**—Creativity; autonomy; responsibility; achievement; ability utilization. **Work Conditions**—Sitting; outdoors, exposed to weather; very hot or cold; indoors, environmentally controlled.

Archeology

Focuses on the systematic study of extinct societies, and the past of living societies, via the excavation, analysis and interpretation of their artifactual, human, and associated remains. **Related CIP Program:** 45.0301 Archeology.

Specializations in the Major: Ancient civilizations, field work, prehistoric archeology, preservation.

Typical Sequence of College Courses: English composition, statistics for business and social sciences, foreign language, introduction to archeology, world prehistory, ancient literate civilizations, field methods in archeology, new world archeology, seminar (reporting on research). **Typical Sequence**

of High School Courses: Algebra, English, foreign language, social science, history, biology, public speaking.

Career Snapshot: Archeology (also spelled archaeology) is the study of prehistoric and historic cultures through the discovery, preservation, and interpretation of their material remains. As a major, it is sometimes offered as a specialization within anthropology or classics. Students work with languages as well as physical objects, so they develop a number of skills that are appreciated in the business world. They may also get higher degrees in archeology in order to do museum work, field work, or college teaching.

Related Jobs			
Job Title	Average Earnings	Job Growth	Job Openings
1. Anthropology and Archeology Teachers, Postsecondary	$60,190	32.2%	329,000
2. Archeologists	$44,620	17.0%	fewer than 500

Job 1 shares 329,000 job openings with 35 jobs not included in the list.

Characteristics of the Related Jobs: Interests—Investigative; Social; Artistic. **Skills**—Writing; science; active learning; critical thinking; reading comprehension. **Values**—Creativity; autonomy; responsibility; achievement; ability utilization. **Work Conditions**—Sitting; outdoors, exposed to weather; very hot or cold; indoors, environmentally controlled.

Architecture

Prepares individuals for the independent professional practice of architecture and to conduct research in various aspects of the field. **Related CIP Program:** 04.0201 Architecture (B.Arch., B.A./B.S., M.Arch., M.A./M.S., Ph.D.).

Specializations in the Major: Architectural engineering, design, history, theory and criticism, urban studies.

Typical Sequence of College Courses: English composition, basic drawing, art history: Renaissance to modern, calculus, introduction to computer science, general physics, history of architecture, structures, building science, visual analysis of architecture, architectural graphics, architectural design,

© JIST Works

architectural computer graphics, site analysis, introduction to urban planning. **Typical Sequence of High School Courses:** English, algebra, geometry, trigonometry, pre-calculus, calculus, physics, computer science, art.

Career Snapshot: Architects design buildings and the spaces between them. They must have a combination of artistic, technical, and business skills. In order to be licensed, they must obtain a professional degree in architecture (sometimes a five-year bachelor's degree, sometimes a master's degree after a bachelor's in another field); work as an intern, typically for three years; and pass a licensing exam. About one-third are self-employed, and most architectural firms are quite small. Computer skills can be a big advantage for new graduates. Best internship opportunities will be for those who have interned while still in school. Demand for architectural services depends on the amount of building construction and therefore varies with economic ups and downs and by geographic region.

Related Jobs			
Job Title	Average Earnings	Job Growth	Job Openings
1. Architects, Except Landscape and Naval	$61,430	17.3%	7,000
2. Architecture Teachers, Postsecondary	$60,400	32.2%	329,000
3. Engineering Managers	$99,000	13.0%	15,000

Job 2 shares 329,000 job openings with 35 jobs not included in the list.

Characteristics of the Related Jobs: Interests—Enterprising; Realistic; Investigative. **Skills**—Operations analysis; management of financial resources; technology design; negotiation; science. **Values**—Creativity; authority; compensation; ability utilization; recognition. **Work Conditions**—Common protective or safety equipment; sitting; extremely bright or inadequate lighting; noise levels are distracting or uncomfortable; high places.

Area Studies

Focuses on the history, society, politics, culture, and economics of one or more of the peoples of a geographical region, such as Africa, the United States, Asia, the Caribbean, Latin America, the Middle East, and so forth. **Related CIP Programs:** 05.0101 African Studies; 05.0102 American/ United States Studies/Civilization; 05.0103 Asian Studies/Civilization; 05.0116 Balkans Studies; 05.0117 Baltic Studies; 05.0115 Canadian Studies; 05.0119 Caribbean Studies; 05.0105 Central/Middle and Eastern European Studies; 05.0123 Chinese Studies; 05.0121 Commonwealth Studies; 05.0104 East Asian Studies; 05.0106 European Studies/ Civilization; 05.0124 French Studies; 05.0125 German Studies; 05.0126 Italian Studies; 05.0127 Japanese Studies; 05.0128 Korean Studies; 05.0107 Latin American Studies; 05.0108 Near and Middle Eastern Studies; 05.0109 Pacific Area/Pacific Rim Studies; 05.0129 Polish Studies; 05.0122 Regional Studies (U.S., Canadian, Foreign); 05.0110 Russian Studies; 05.0111 Scandinavian Studies; 05.0118 Slavic Studies; 05.0112 South Asian Studies; 05.0113 Southeast Asian Studies; 05.0130 Spanish and Iberian Studies; 05.0131 Tibetan Studies; 05.0132 Ukraine Studies; 05.0120 Ural-Altaic and Central Asian Studies; 05.0114 Western European Studies.

Specializations in the Major: Economics and trade, history and culture, language and literature, political science.

Typical Sequence of College Courses: English composition, foreign language, foreign literature and culture, comparative governments, introduction to economics, international economics, seminar (reporting on research). **Typical Sequence of High School Courses:** English, foreign language, history, literature, social science, algebra.

Career Snapshot: Certain very popular area studies—African-American studies, American studies, and women's studies—are described elsewhere in this book. But many colleges offer other area studies majors, usually defined in terms of a region of the world: East Asian studies, European studies, Latin American studies, and so on. These are interdisciplinary majors that may involve some combination of linguistics, literature, history, sociology, political science, economic development, or other disciplines. Usually you can emphasize whichever aspects interest you most. Graduates of area studies may go into a business or government career where knowledge of a foreign culture is an advantage. Many get higher degrees to prepare for a career in law or college teaching.

© JIST Works

	Related Job		
Job Title	Average Earnings	Job Growth	Job Openings
Area, Ethnic, and Cultural Studies Teachers, Postsecondary	$55,660	32.2%	329,000

This job shares 329,000 job openings with 35 jobs not included in the list.

Characteristics of the Related Job: Interests—Social; Investigative; Artistic. **Skills**—Writing; instructing; critical thinking; persuasion; active learning. **Values**—Authority; social service; creativity; achievement; social status. **Work Conditions**—Sitting; indoors, environmentally controlled.

Art

Focuses on the introductory study and appreciation of the visual arts, and prepares individuals to generally function as creative artists in the visual and plastic media. **Related CIP Programs:** 50.0701 Art/Art Studies, General; 50.0711 Ceramic Arts and Ceramics; 50.0705 Drawing; 50.0712 Fiber, Textile, and Weaving Arts; 50.0702 Fine/Studio Arts, General; 50.0706 Intermedia/Multimedia; 50.0713 Metal and Jewelry Arts; 50.0708 Painting; 50.0710 Printmaking; 50.0709 Sculpture.

Specializations in the Major: Art education, ceramics, painting, screen-printing, sculpture, studio art.

Typical Sequence of College Courses: English composition, foreign language, art and culture, basic drawing, color and design, two-dimensional design, three-dimensional design, art history: prehistoric to Renaissance, art history: Renaissance to modern, figure drawing, a medium (e.g., painting, sculpture, ceramics), art practicum. **Typical Sequence of High School Courses:** English, foreign language, literature, history, art.

Career Snapshot: Only a few highly talented and motivated artists are able to support themselves by producing and selling their artwork. But many other graduates of art programs find work in education—as private instructors, school teachers, and university instructors of art and art history. College teaching requires a master's degree. Some graduates apply their artistic skills to crafts or to commercial applications such as illustration or cartooning.

Related Jobs			
Job Title	Average Earnings	Job Growth	Job Openings
1. Art Directors	$63,750	11.5%	10,000
2. Art, Drama, and Music Teachers, Postsecondary	$49,740	32.2%	329,000
3. Cartoonists	$41,240	10.2%	4,000
4. Multi-Media Artists and Animators	$49,900	14.1%	14,000
5. Painters and Illustrators	$41,240	10.2%	4,000
6. Sculptors	$41,240	10.2%	4,000
7. Sketch Artists	$41,240	10.2%	4,000

Job 2 shares 329,000 job openings with 35 jobs not included in the list. Jobs 3, 5, 6, and 7 share 4,000 job openings.

Characteristics of the Related Jobs: Interests—Artistic; Social; Investigative. **Skills**—Persuasion; instructing; active listening; time management; speaking. **Values**—Creativity; ability utilization; achievement; autonomy; authority. **Work Conditions**—Sitting; indoors, environmentally controlled; spend time making repetitive motions.

Art History

Focuses on the study of the historical development of art as social and intellectual phenomenon, the analysis of works of art, and art conservation. **Related CIP Program:** 50.0703 Art History, Criticism and Conservation.

Specializations in the Major: A historical period, a particular artistic medium, a region of the world, criticism.

Typical Sequence of College Courses: English composition; foreign language; art and culture; studio art; world history to the early modern era; world history in the modern era; art history: prehistoric to Renaissance, Renaissance to modern, non-Western art, critical study of visual art.
Typical Sequence of High School Courses: English, art, foreign language, history, literature, social science.

© JIST Works

Career Snapshot: Art has been important to humans since people painted on cave walls, and art history majors learn how art forms, techniques, and traditions have developed since then within their historical and cultural contexts. Study abroad is often part of the curriculum. Graduates of art history programs with a bachelor's degree may work for museums, auction houses, or publishers. With additional education or training, they may work as college teachers or restorers.

	Related Jobs		
Job Title	**Average Earnings**	**Job Growth**	**Job Openings**
1. Archivists	$37,500	13.4%	1,000
2. Art, Drama, and Music Teachers, Postsecondary	$49,740	32.2%	329,000
3. Curators	$43,920	15.7%	1,000
4. Museum Technicians and Conservators	$32,860	14.1%	2,000

Job 2 shares 329,000 job openings with 35 jobs not included in the list.

Characteristics of the Related Jobs: Interests—Artistic; Social; Investigative. **Skills**—Instructing; persuasion; social perceptiveness; speaking; learning strategies. **Values**—Authority; social service; creativity; ability utilization; working conditions. **Work Conditions**—Indoors, environmentally controlled; sitting.

Astronomy

Focuses on the planetary, galactic, and stellar phenomena occurring in outer space. **Related CIP Programs:** 40.0201 Astronomy; 40.0202 Astrophysics; 40.0203 Planetary Astronomy and Science.

Specializations in the Major: Astrophysics, cosmology.

Typical Sequence of College Courses: English composition, introduction to computer science, calculus, differential equations, general chemistry, general physics, mechanics, electricity and magnetism, thermal physics, introduction to astrophysics, astrophysical processes, quantum and atomic physics, observational astronomy. **Typical Sequence of High School Courses:** English, algebra, geometry, trigonometry, chemistry, physics, pre-calculus, computer science, calculus.

Career Snapshot: Almost every year, astronomers make important discoveries that challenge existing theories about the planets, stars, and galaxies and the forces that formed them. Astronomers typically spend only a small fraction of their time actually observing, and much more time analyzing data and comparing it to theoretical models. Many are college faculty members with teaching responsibilities. A Ph.D. is the usual requirement for astronomers, and many new Ph.D.s find a postdoctoral research appointment helpful for future employment. The occupation has only a small workforce, and some graduates of astronomy programs apply their skills to more earthbound pursuits, such as research and development in private industry.

Related Jobs			
Job Title	Average Earnings	Job Growth	Job Openings
1. Astronomers	$99,120	10.4%	fewer than 500
2. Atmospheric, Earth, Marine, and Space Sciences Teachers, Postsecondary	$65,250	32.2%	329,000
3. Natural Sciences Managers	$90,080	13.6%	5,000
4. Physicists	$87,480	7.0%	1,000

Job 2 shares 329,000 job openings with 35 jobs not included in the list.

Characteristics of the Related Jobs: Interests—Investigative; Enterprising; Realistic. **Skills**—Science; mathematics; active learning; writing; management of personnel resources. **Values**—Creativity; authority; autonomy; working conditions; responsibility. **Work Conditions**—Indoors, environmentally controlled; sitting.

Biochemistry

Focuses on the scientific study of the chemistry of living systems, their fundamental chemical substances and reactions, and their chemical pathways and information transfer systems, with particular reference to carbohy-drates, proteins, lipids, and nucleic acids. **Related CIP Program:** 26.0202 Biochemistry.

Specializations in the Major: Forensic chemistry, pharmacological chem-istry, recombinant DNA, research.

Typical Sequence of College Courses: English composition, calculus, intro-duction to computer science, general chemistry, general biology, organic chemistry, general physics, analytical chemistry, general microbiology, intro-duction to biochemistry, cell biology, molecular biology, physical chemistry, genetics. **Typical Sequence of High School Courses:** English, algebra, trigonometry, biology, geometry, chemistry, physics, computer science, pre-calculus, calculus.

Career Snapshot: Biochemistry studies the fundamental chemical processes that support life. The recent growth of the pharmaceutical industry and of genetic engineering technology has fueled the demand for biochemistry majors, especially at the graduate level, but there will be a lot of competi-tion for independent research positions that are supported by grants—as are many university jobs. Better opportunities are expected for those with bachelor's degrees who seek work in nonresearch jobs such as sales, market-ing, and clinical laboratory testing.

Related Jobs			
Job Title	Average Earnings	Job Growth	Job Openings
1. Biochemists	$68,700	21.0%	1,000
2. Biological Science Teachers, Postsecondary	$63,750	32.2%	329,000
3. Medical Scientists, Except Epidemiologists	$60,240	34.1%	15,000
4. Natural Sciences Managers	$90,080	13.6%	5,000

Job 1 shares 1,000 job openings with another job not included in the list. Job 2 shares 329,000 job open-ings with 35 jobs not included in the list.

Characteristics of the Related Jobs: Interest—Investigative. **Skills**—Science; reading comprehension; writing; active learning; critical thinking. **Values**—Creativity; social status; authority; autonomy; ability utilization. **Work Conditions**—Indoors, environmentally controlled; exposed to disease or infections; hazardous conditions; sitting.

Bioengineering

Prepares individuals to apply mathematical and scientific principles to the design, development, and operational evaluation of systems, equipment, and facilities used to produce, process, and store agricultural products; to improve the productivity of agricultural methods; and to develop improved agricultural biological systems. **Related CIP Program:** 14.0301 Agricultural/Biological Engineering and Bioengineering.

Specializations in the Major: Biomechanics, biomedical engineering, computational bioengineering, controlled drug delivery, engineered biomaterials, medical imaging, molecular bioengineering, prosthetics and artificial organs.

Typical Sequence of College Courses: English composition, technical writing, calculus, differential equations, general chemistry, introduction to computer science, general physics, introduction to electric circuits, general biology, mechanics, introduction to bioengineering, bioinstrumentation, biomaterials, biomechanics, business information processing. **Typical Sequence of High School Courses:** English, algebra, geometry, trigonometry, pre-calculus, calculus, chemistry, biology, physics, computer science.

Career Snapshot: Bioengineering uses engineering principles of analysis and design to solve problems in medicine and biology. It finds ways to improve health care, agriculture, and industrial processes. Graduates with a bachelor's may work in industry, but increasing competition is making an advanced degree more important and it is needed to prepare for a career in research or college teaching. Some graduates go on to medical school. This is one of the fastest-moving fields in engineering, so people in this field need to learn continuously to keep up with new technologies.

© JIST Works

Related Jobs			
Job Title	Average Earnings	Job Growth	Job Openings
1. Agricultural Engineers	$60,340	12.0%	fewer than 500
2. Engineering Managers	$99,000	13.0%	15,000
3. Engineering Teachers, Postsecondary	$74,840	32.2%	329,000

Job 3 shares 329,000 job openings with 35 jobs not included in the list.

Characteristics of the Related Jobs: Interests—Enterprising; Investigative; Realistic. **Skills**—Technology design; science; operations analysis; management of financial resources; installation. **Values**—Authority; creativity; autonomy; compensation; ability utilization. **Work Conditions**—Common protective or safety equipment; noise levels are distracting or uncomfortable; hazardous equipment; extremely bright or inadequate lighting; sitting.

Biology

Focuses on biology at the introductory, basic level or a program in biology or the biological sciences. **Related CIP Program:** 26.0101 Biology/ Biological Sciences, General.

Specializations in the Major: Biochemistry, botany, cell biology, ecology, genetics, microbiology, zoology.

Typical Sequence of College Courses: English composition, calculus, introduction to computer science, general chemistry, statistics, general biology, organic chemistry, genetics, general physics, cell biology, introduction to biochemistry, general microbiology, ecology, organisms and populations, animal anatomy and physiology, plant anatomy. **Typical Sequence of High School Courses:** Algebra, English, biology, geometry, trigonometry, chemistry, physics, pre-calculus, computer science, calculus.

Career Snapshot: Although it is often possible to study a specialization— such as botany, zoology, or biochemistry—many colleges offer a major in the general field of biology. With a bachelor's degree in biology, one may work as a technician or entry-level researcher in a medical, pharmaceutical, or governmental regulatory setting, or as a sales representative in a technical field such as pharmaceuticals. Such job opportunities are expected to be good. Teaching biology in high school or middle school almost always requires additional coursework (perhaps a master's) in teaching theory and methods, plus supervised classroom experience. A large number of biology majors go on to pursue graduate or professional degrees and thus prepare for careers as researchers, college teachers, physicians, dentists, and veterinarians.

Related Jobs			
Job Title	Average Earnings	Job Growth	Job Openings
1. Biological Science Teachers, Postsecondary	$63,750	32.2%	329,000
2. Natural Sciences Managers	$90,080	13.6%	5,000

Job 1 shares 329,000 job openings with 35 jobs not included in the list.

Characteristics of the Related Jobs: Interests—Investigative; Social; Enterprising. **Skills**—Science; instructing; active learning; reading comprehension; writing. **Values**—Authority; creativity; social service; social status; responsibility. **Work Conditions**—Hazardous conditions; indoors, environmentally controlled; contaminants; exposed to disease or infections; sitting.

Botany

Focuses on the scientific study of plants, related microbial organisms, and plant habitats and ecosystem relations. **Related CIP Program:** 26.0301 Botany/Plant Biology.

Specializations in the Major: Forestry, phytopathology (plant disease), plant genetics.

Typical Sequence of College Courses: English composition, calculus, introduction to computer science, general chemistry, statistics, general biology, organic chemistry, genetics, general physics, cell biology, introduction to biochemistry, general microbiology, taxonomy of flowering plants, ecology, plant anatomy, plant physiology. **Typical Sequence of High School Courses:** English, algebra, biology, geometry, trigonometry, chemistry, physics, pre-calculus, computer science, calculus.

© JIST Works

Career Snapshot: Botany is the science of plants. Because all of our food resources and the very air we breathe ultimately depend on the growth of plants, botany is a vital field of knowledge. A bachelor's degree in this field prepares you for some non-research jobs in industry, agriculture, forestry, and environmental protection. Best opportunities are in agricultural research, where a graduate degree is expected.

Related Jobs			
Job Title	Average Earnings	Job Growth	Job Openings
1. Biological Science Teachers, Postsecondary	$63,750	32.2%	329,000
2. Natural Sciences Managers	$90,080	13.6%	5,000

Job 1 shares 329,000 job openings with 35 jobs not included in the list.

Characteristics of the Related Jobs: Interests—Investigative; Social; Enterprising. **Skills**—Science; instructing; active learning; reading comprehension; writing. **Values**—Authority; creativity; social service; social status; responsibility. **Work Conditions**—Hazardous conditions; indoors, environmentally controlled; contaminants; exposed to disease or infections; sitting.

Business Education

Prepares individuals to teach vocational business programs at various educational levels. **Related CIP Program:** 13.1303 Business Teacher Education.

Specializations in the Major: Distributive education, office skills.

Typical Sequence of College Courses: Introduction to psychology, English composition, oral communication, history and philosophy of education, human growth and development, introduction to accounting, legal environment of business, introduction to business management, business math, business information processing, keyboarding, statistics, business reports and communication, introduction to marketing, methods of teaching business subjects, student teaching. **Typical Sequence of High School Courses:** English, algebra, geometry, trigonometry, science, foreign language, keyboarding, office computer applications, public speaking.

Career Snapshot: Business educators teach secondary school students skills and knowledge they will need to succeed in the business world. Therefore, they must know about one or more specific business fields—such as bookkeeping, retailing, or office computer applications—as well as about techniques for teaching and for managing the classroom. A bachelor's degree is often an entry route to the first teaching job, but job security and pay raises often require a master's degree.

Related Jobs			
Job Title	Average Earnings	Job Growth	Job Openings
1. Business Teachers, Postsecondary	$58,230	32.2%	329,000
2. Education Teachers, Postsecondary	$50,410	32.2%	329,000
3. Secondary School Teachers, Except Special and Vocational Education	$46,120	14.4%	107,000
4. Vocational Education Teachers, Postsecondary	$41,170	32.2%	329,000

Jobs 1, 2, and 4 share 329,000 job openings with each other and with 33 jobs not included in the list.

Characteristics of the Related Jobs: Interest—Social. **Skills**—Learning strategies; instructing; social perceptiveness; persuasion; monitoring. **Values**—Social service; authority; creativity; responsibility; achievement. **Work Conditions**—Standing; noise levels are distracting or uncomfortable; indoors, environmentally controlled.

Business Management

Prepares individuals to plan, organize, direct, and control the functions and processes of a firm or organization. **Related CIP Program:** 52.0201 Business Administration and Management, General.

Specializations in the Major: International business, management, marketing, operations.

© JIST Works

Typical Sequence of College Courses: English composition, business writing, introduction to psychology, principles of microeconomics, principles of macroeconomics, calculus for business and social sciences, statistics for business and social sciences, introduction to management information systems, introduction to accounting, legal environment of business, principles of management and organization, operations management, strategic management, business finance, introduction to marketing, organizational behavior, human resource management, international management, organizational theory. **Typical Sequence of High School Courses:** English, algebra, geometry, trigonometry, science, foreign language, computer science, public speaking.

Career Snapshot: Students of business management learn about the principles of economics, the legal and social environment in which business operates, and quantitative methods for measuring and projecting business activity. Graduates may enter the business world directly or pursue a master's degree. Some get a bachelor's degree in a nonbusiness field and enter a master's of business administration program after getting some entry-level work experience.

Related Jobs			
Job Title	*Average Earnings*	*Job Growth*	*Job Openings*
1. Administrative Services Managers	$62,300	16.9%	25,000
2. Business Teachers, Postsecondary	$58,230	32.2%	329,000
3. Chief Executives	$141,820	14.9%	38,000
4. Construction Managers	$70,770	10.4%	28,000
5. Cost Estimators	$50,920	18.2%	15,000
6. General and Operations Managers	$79,300	17.0%	208,000
7. Industrial Production Managers	$74,100	0.8%	13,000
8. Management Analysts	$64,560	20.1%	82,000
9. Private Sector Executives	$141,820	14.9%	38,000
10. Sales Managers	$85,980	19.7%	40,000

Job 2 shares 329,000 job openings with 35 jobs not included in the list. Job 9 shares 38,000 job openings with another job not included in the list.

Characteristics of the Related Jobs: Interests—Enterprising; Conventional; Social. **Skills**—Management of financial resources; management of personnel resources; negotiation; management of material resources; monitoring. **Values**—Authority; creativity; autonomy; responsibility; compensation. **Work Conditions**—Indoors, environmentally controlled.

Chemical Engineering

Prepares individuals to apply mathematical and scientific principles to the design, development, and operational evaluation of systems employing chemical processes. **Related CIP Program:** 14.0701 Chemical Engineering.

Specializations in the Major: Bioengineering, nuclear engineering, pharmaceuticals, quality control.

Typical Sequence of College Courses: English composition, technical writing, calculus, differential equations, general chemistry, general physics, introduction to computer science, introduction to electric circuits, organic chemistry, introduction to chemical engineering, thermodynamics, numerical analysis, materials engineering, chemical engineering thermodynamics, kinetics and reactor design, mass transfer operations, plant design, process dynamics and controls, process design and optimization, senior design project. **Typical Sequence of High School Courses:** English, algebra, geometry, trigonometry, pre-calculus, calculus, chemistry, physics, computer science.

Career Snapshot: Chemical engineers apply principles of chemistry to solve engineering problems, such as how to prepare large batches of chemical compounds economically, with uniform consistency and quality. A bachelor's degree is the usual entry route for this field. Among manufacturing industries, best opportunities are expected in pharmaceuticals, but most job growth is expected in research and development. Engineers often move on to managerial jobs.

Related Jobs			
Job Title	Average Earnings	Job Growth	Job Openings
1. Chemical Engineers	$76,500	10.6%	3,000
2. Engineering Managers	$99,000	13.0%	15,000
3. Engineering Teachers, Postsecondary	$74,840	32.2%	329,000

Job 3 shares 329,000 job openings with 35 jobs not included in the list.

© JIST Works

Characteristics of the Related Jobs: Interests—Enterprising; Investigative; Realistic. **Skills**—Technology design; science; operations analysis; management of financial resources; installation. **Values**—Authority; creativity; autonomy; compensation; ability utilization. **Work Conditions**—Common protective or safety equipment; noise levels are distracting or uncomfortable; sitting; hazardous equipment; extremely bright or inadequate lighting.

Chemistry

Focuses on the scientific study of the composition and behavior of matter, including its micro- and macro-structure, the processes of chemical change, and the theoretical description and laboratory simulation of these phenomena. **Related CIP Program:** 40.0501 Chemistry, General.

Specializations in the Major: Forensic chemistry, geological/ocean chemistry, quality control, research.

Typical Sequence of College Courses: English composition, calculus, introduction to computer science, general chemistry, molecular structure and bonding, organic chemistry, qualitative analysis, quantitative analysis, general physics, statistics, physical chemistry, inorganic chemistry, undergraduate research project. **Typical Sequence of High School Courses:** English, algebra, geometry, trigonometry, pre-calculus, calculus, chemistry, physics, computer science.

Career Snapshot: Everything around us and within us is composed of chemicals, and chemists search for and put to use new knowledge about the nature and properties of matter. Chemists develop new fibers, paints, pharmaceuticals, solvents, fuels, and countless other materials that are used in industry and the home. A bachelor's degree is usually required for entry to this field, but a Ph.D. is often needed for research or college teaching. Best job opportunities and the greatest security are expected in companies that manufacture pharmaceuticals or do chemical testing. Companies that provide chemicals for industrial purposes are more sensitive to economic ups and downs. Some bachelor's degree holders find work in sales, marketing, or middle management in companies that value knowledge of chemistry.

Related Jobs			
Job Title	Average Earnings	Job Growth	Job Openings
1. Chemistry Teachers, Postsecondary	$57,340	32.2%	329,000
2. Chemists	$57,090	7.3%	5,000
3. Natural Sciences Managers	$90,080	13.6%	5,000

Job 1 shares 329,000 job openings with 35 jobs not included in the list.

Characteristics of the Related Jobs: Interests—Investigative; Realistic; Conventional. **Skills**—Science; technology design; active learning; time management; management of financial resources. **Values**—Creativity; ability utilization; responsibility; autonomy; achievement. **Work Conditions**—Hazardous conditions; common protective or safety equipment; contaminants; indoors, environmentally controlled; specialized protective or safety equipment.

Chinese

Focuses on the Chinese language and its associated dialects and literature; includes the cultural and historical contexts and applications to business, science/technology, and other settings. **Related CIP Program:** 16.0301 Chinese Language and Literature.

Specializations in the Major: History and culture, language education, literature, translation.

Typical Sequence of College Courses: Chinese language, conversation, composition, linguistics, Chinese literature, East Asian literature, East Asian studies, grammar, phonetics. **Typical Sequence of High School Courses:** English, public speaking, foreign language, history, literature, social science.

Career Snapshot: Because Chinese is spoken by more people than any other language, there is a growing need for Americans with knowledge of the Chinese language and culture, especially now that U.S. trade with China is so intense. A bachelor's degree in Chinese, perhaps with additional education in business or law, may lead to an Asia-centered career in business or government. A graduate degree is good preparation for translation or college teaching.

© JIST Works

Related Jobs			
Job Title	Average Earnings	Job Growth	Job Openings
1. Foreign Language and Literature Teachers, Postsecondary	$49,120	32.2%	329,000
2. Interpreters and Translators	$34,900	19.9%	4,000

Job 1 shares 329,000 job openings with 35 jobs not included in the list.

Characteristics of the Related Jobs: Interests—Artistic; Social; Investigative. **Skills**—Writing; active listening; speaking; reading comprehension; service orientation. **Values**—Social service; ability utilization; achievement; autonomy; social status. **Work Conditions**—Sitting; indoors, environmentally controlled.

Chiropractic

Prepares individuals for the independent professional practice of chiropractics, a health care and healing system based on the application of non-invasive treatments and spinal adjustments to alleviate health problems caused by vertebral misalignments affecting bodily function as derived from the philosophy of Daniel Palmer. **Related CIP Program:** 51.0101 Chiropractic (DC).

Specializations in the Major: Diagnostic imaging, orthopedics, sports medicine.

Typical Sequence of College Courses: English composition, introduction to psychology, college algebra, calculus, introduction to sociology, oral communication, general chemistry, general biology, introduction to computer science, organic chemistry, human anatomy and physiology, general microbiology, genetics, introduction to biochemistry, veterinary gross anatomy, spinal anatomy, histology, biomechanics, physical diagnosis, neuroanatomy, neurophysiology, radiographic anatomy, emergency care, nutrition, neuromusculoskeletal diagnosis and treatment, chiropractic manipulative therapeutics, pathology, public health, patient examination and evaluation, pharmacology, minor surgery, clinical experience in obstetrics/gynecology, clinical experience in pediatrics, clinical experience in geriatrics, mental health, ethics in health care, professional practice management. **Typical Sequence of High School Courses:** English, algebra, geometry, trigonometry, biology, computer science, public speaking, chemistry, foreign language, physics, pre-calculus.

Career Snapshot: Chiropractors are health practitioners who specialize in health problems associated with the muscular, nervous, and skeletal systems, especially the spine. They learn a variety of specialized diagnostic and treatment techniques but also tend to emphasize the patient's overall health and wellness, recommending changes in diet and lifestyle that can help the body's own healing powers. The educational program includes not only theory and laboratory work, but also a lot of supervised clinical work with patients. With the aging of the population and increased acceptance of chiropractic medicine, job opportunities for graduates are expected to be good.

Related Jobs			
Job Title	**Average Earnings**	**Job Growth**	**Job Openings**
1. Chiropractors	$67,940	22.4%	4,000
2. Health Specialties Teachers, Postsecondary	$70,310	32.2%	329,000

Job 2 shares 329,000 job openings with 35 jobs not included in the list.

Characteristics of the Related Jobs: Interests—Investigative; Social; Artistic. **Skills**—Science; instructing; learning strategies; writing; critical thinking. **Values**—Social service; authority; creativity; social status; achievement. **Work Conditions**—Exposed to disease or infections; indoors, environmentally controlled; sitting; exposed to radiation.

Civil Engineering

Prepares individuals to apply mathematical and scientific principles to the design, development, and operational evaluation of structural, load-bearing, material moving, transportation, water resource, and material control systems; and environmental safety measures. **Related CIP Program:** 14.0801 Civil Engineering, General.

Specializations in the Major: Environmental engineering, geotechnical engineering, structural engineering, transportation engineering, water resources.

© JIST Works

Typical Sequence of College Courses: English composition, technical writing, calculus, differential equations, general chemistry, introduction to computer science, general physics, introduction to electric circuits, engineering graphics, statics, dynamics, materials engineering, introduction to civil engineering, numerical analysis, fluid mechanics, engineering surveying and measurement, environmental engineering and design, soil mechanics, engineering economics, analysis of structures, highway and transportation engineering, reinforced concrete design, steel design, water resources and hydraulic engineering, senior design project. **Typical Sequence of High School Courses:** English, algebra, geometry, trigonometry, pre-calculus, calculus, chemistry, physics, computer science.

Career Snapshot: Civil engineers design and supervise construction of roads, buildings, bridges, dams, airports, water-supply systems, and many other projects that affect the quality of our environment. They apply principles of physics and other sciences to devise engineering solutions that are technically effective, as well as being economically and environmentally sound. A bachelor's degree is the usual way to enter the field. Engineering is also a good way to prepare for a later position in management. Employment opportunities tend to rise and fall with the economy.

Related Jobs			
Job Title	Average Earnings	Job Growth	Job Openings
1. Civil Engineers	$65,280	16.5%	19,000
2. Engineering Managers	$99,000	13.0%	15,000
3. Engineering Teachers, Postsecondary	$74,840	32.2%	329,000

Job 3 shares 329,000 job openings with 35 jobs not included in the list.

Characteristics of the Related Jobs: Interests—Realistic; Investigative; Enterprising. **Skills**—Science; operations analysis; technology design; persuasion; mathematics. **Values**—Authority; creativity; autonomy; ability utilization; social status. **Work Conditions**—Outdoors, exposed to weather; very hot or cold; sitting; hazardous equipment; contaminants.

Classics

Focuses on the Greek and Latin languages and their literatures during ancient times; includes the cultural and historical contexts, dialects, and applications to business, science/technology, and other settings. **Related CIP Programs:** 16.1202 Ancient/Classical Greek Language and Literature; 16.1200 Classics and Classical Languages, Literatures, and Linguistics, General; 16.1203 Latin Language and Literature.

Specializations in the Major: Archeology, classical civilization, classical linguistics, classical literature/mythology, Greek, Latin.

Typical Sequence of College Courses: Latin, Greek, grammar, linguistics, literature of the Roman Empire, literature in ancient Greek, history of the ancient world. **Typical Sequence of High School Courses:** English, public speaking, foreign language, history, literature, social science.

Career Snapshot: The classical languages—Latin and Greek—may be dead, but students who study them often end up in very lively careers. The mental discipline and critical-thinking skills learned in the classics can be first-rate preparation for law school and medical school, and business recruiters report that classics graduates have an exceptional breadth of view. The demand for Latin teachers in secondary schools is strong. A classics major is also a good first step to graduate training in archeology, history, or theology.

Related Jobs			
Job Title	**Average Earnings**	**Job Growth**	**Job Openings**
1. Foreign Language and Literature Teachers, Postsecondary	$49,120	32.2%	329,000
2. Interpreters and Translators	$34,900	19.9%	4,000

Job 1 shares 329,000 job openings with 35 jobs not included in the list.

Characteristics of the Related Jobs: Interests—Artistic; Social; Investigative. **Skills**—Writing; active listening; speaking; reading comprehension; service orientation. **Values**—Social service; ability utilization; achievement; autonomy; social status. **Work Conditions**—Sitting; indoors, environmentally controlled.

© JIST Works

Communications Studies/Speech

Focuses on the scientific, humanistic, and critical study of human communication in a variety of formats, media, and contexts. **Related CIP Program:** 09.0101 Communication Studies/Speech Communication and Rhetoric.

Specializations in the Major: Business communications, speech/rhetoric.

Typical Sequence of College Courses: Public speaking, introduction to psychology, English composition, communications theory, introduction to mass communication, argumentation and critical thinking, interpersonal communication, rhetorical tradition and techniques. **Typical Sequence of High School Courses:** English, public speaking, foreign language, applied communications, social science.

Career Snapshot: This major is sometimes offered in the same department as mass communications or theater, but it is not designed to teach a technical skill such as television production or acting. Instead, it teaches how effective communication depends on a combination of verbal and nonverbal elements. Students work in various media and learn how to strike a balance among covering the subject matter, appealing to the listener or reader, and projecting the intended image of the speaker or writer. Graduates of communication and speech programs may go on to careers in sales, public relations, law, or teaching.

Related Jobs			
Job Title	*Average Earnings*	*Job Growth*	*Job Openings*
1. Caption Writers	$45,460	17.7%	14,000
2. Communications Teachers, Postsecondary	$50,610	32.2%	329,000
3. Copy Writers	$45,460	17.7%	14,000
4. Creative Writers	$45,460	17.7%	14,000
5. Editors	$44,390	22.9%	38,000
6. Poets and Lyricists	$45,460	17.7%	14,000
7. Public Address System and Other Announcers	$22,390	3.8%	2,000
8. Writers and Authors	$54,390	23.2%	5,000

Jobs 1, 3, 4, and 6 share 14,000 job openings. Job 2 shares 329,000 job openings with 35 jobs not included in the list.

Characteristics of the Related Jobs: Interests—Artistic; Social; Enterprising. Skills—Writing; reading comprehension; monitoring; persuasion; time management. Values—Creativity; ability utilization; recognition; achievement; autonomy. Work Conditions—Sitting; indoors, environmentally controlled.

Computer Engineering

Prepares individuals to apply mathematical and scientific principles to the design, development, and operational evaluation of computer hardware and software systems and related equipment and facilities; and the analysis of specific problems of computer applications to various tasks. Related CIP Program: 14.0901 Computer Engineering, General.

Specializations in the Major: Hardware design, software/systems design, systems analysis.

Typical Sequence of College Courses: English composition, technical writing, calculus, differential equations, general chemistry, introduction to computer science, general physics, introduction to engineering, introduction to electric circuits, engineering circuit analysis, numerical analysis, electrical networks, electronics, computer architecture, algorithms and data structures, digital system design, software engineering, operating systems, microcomputer systems, senior design project. Typical Sequence of High School Courses: English, algebra, geometry, trigonometry, pre-calculus, calculus, chemistry, physics, computer science.

Career Snapshot: Computer engineers use their knowledge of scientific principles to design computers, networks of computers, and systems (such as telecommunications) that include computers. They need to understand both hardware and software, and they may build prototypes of new systems. The usual entry route is via a bachelor's degree. Opportunities for employment are good despite foreign competition, especially in nonmanufacturing jobs related to systems design. Some engineers go into management, and the computer industry provides many opportunities for creative and motivated engineers to become entrepreneurs.

Related Jobs			
Job Title	Average Earnings	Job Growth	Job Openings
1. Computer Hardware Engineers	$82,750	10.1%	5,000

© JIST Works

2. Computer Software Engineers, Applications	$76,310	48.4%	54,000
3. Computer Software Engineers, Systems Software	$81,140	43.0%	37,000
4. Engineering Managers	$99,000	13.0%	15,000
5. Engineering Teachers, Postsecondary	$74,840	32.2%	329,000

Job 5 shares 329,000 job openings with 35 jobs not included in the list.

Characteristics of the Related Jobs: Interests—Investigative; Realistic; Conventional. **Skills**—Programming; technology design; troubleshooting; operations analysis; systems analysis. **Values**—Creativity; ability utilization; authority; working conditions; responsibility. **Work Conditions**—Sitting; indoors, environmentally controlled; spend time making repetitive motions.

Computer Science

Focuses on computers, computing problems and solutions, and the design of computer systems and user interfaces from a scientific perspective. **Related CIP Programs:** 11.0701 Computer Science; 11.0802 Data Modeling/Warehousing and Database Administration.

Specializations in the Major: Business programming, database programming, programming for the Internet, scientific programming, security and disaster recovery, systems programming.

Typical Sequence of College Courses: English composition, calculus, introduction to economics, statistics for business and social sciences, introduction to computer science, programming in a language (e.g., C, PASCAL, COBOL), algorithms and data structures, software engineering, operating systems, database systems, theory of computer languages, computer architecture, artificial intelligence. **Typical Sequence of High School Courses:** English, algebra, geometry, trigonometry, pre-calculus, calculus, chemistry, physics, computer science.

Career Snapshot: Computer science teaches you not only specific languages, but the principles by which languages are created, the structures used to store data, and the logical structures by which programs solve problems. Job outlook is best for roles that are not easily outsourced to overseas workers, such as systems administration and information security.

Related Jobs			
Job Title	Average Earnings	Job Growth	Job Openings
1. Computer and Information Systems Managers	$94,390	25.9%	25,000
2. Computer Science Teachers, Postsecondary	$53,520	32.2%	329,000
3. Computer Software Engineers, Applications	$76,310	48.4%	54,000
4. Computer Software Engineers, Systems Software	$81,140	43.0%	37,000
5. Database Administrators	$61,950	38.2%	9,000

Job 2 shares 329,000 job openings with 35 jobs not included in the list.

Characteristics of the Related Jobs: Interests—Investigative; Realistic; Conventional. **Skills**—Programming; troubleshooting; technology design; systems analysis; operations analysis. **Values**—Creativity; authority; ability utilization; working conditions; responsibility. **Work Conditions**—Sitting; spend time making repetitive motions; indoors, environmentally controlled.

Criminal Justice/Law Enforcement

Prepares individuals to perform the duties of police and public security officers, including patrol and investigative activities, traffic control, crowd control and public relations, witness interviewing, evidence collection and management, basic crime prevention methods, weapon and equipment operation and maintenance, report preparation, and other routine law enforcement responsibilities. **Related CIP Program:** 43.0107 Criminal Justice/Police Science.

Specializations in the Major: Business security, homeland security, police administration, police work.

Typical Sequence of College Courses: Technical writing, introduction to criminal justice, introduction to psychology, American government, criminal law, criminal investigation, introduction to sociology, police organization and administration, criminal procedures, police-community relations,

© JIST Works

ethics, diversity and conflict, seminar (reporting on research). **Typical Sequence of High School Courses:** Algebra, English, foreign language, social science, history, public speaking, computer science.

Career Snapshot: We live in a society that is governed by laws at the municipal, state, and federal levels. These laws are enforced by people who understand the laws themselves, the workings of the agencies that are empowered to enforce them and the techniques for detecting violation of the laws, arresting violators and processing them through the court system. Public concern about crime has created many job opportunities in this field, especially at the local level.

Related Jobs			
Job Title	*Average Earnings*	*Job Growth*	*Job Openings*
1. Bailiffs	$33,720	13.2%	2,000
2. Child Support, Missing Persons, and Unemployment Insurance Fraud Investigators	$54,510	16.3%	9,000
3. Criminal Investigators and Special Agents	$54,510	16.3%	9,000
4. Criminal Justice and Law Enforcement Teachers, Postsecondary	$49,290	32.2%	329,000
5. Highway Patrol Pilots	$45,600	15.5%	47,000
6. Immigration and Customs Inspectors	$54,510	16.3%	9,000
7. Police Detectives	$54,510	16.3%	9,000
8. Police Identification and Records Officers	$54,510	16.3%	9,000
9. Police Patrol Officers	$45,600	15.5%	47,000
10. Private Detectives and Investigators	$32,510	17.7%	7,000

Jobs 2, 3, 6, 7, and 8 share 9,000 job openings. Job 4 shares 329,000 job openings with 35 jobs not included in the list. Jobs 5 and 9 share 47,000 job openings with each other and with another job not included in the list.

Characteristics of the Related Jobs: Interests—Realistic; Enterprising; Social. **Skills**—Social perceptiveness; service orientation; judgment and decision making; persuasion; negotiation. **Values**—Social service; security; authority; achievement; variety. **Work Conditions**—Outdoors, exposed to weather; specialized protective or safety equipment; very hot or cold; common protective or safety equipment; extremely bright or inadequate lighting.

Dance

Prepares individuals to express ideas, feelings, and/or inner visions through the performance of one or more of the dance disciplines, including but not limited to ballet, modern, jazz, ethnic, and folk dance, and that focuses on the study and analysis of dance as a cultural phenomenon. **Related CIP Program:** 50.0301 Dance, General.

Specializations in the Major: Ballet, ballroom dance, composite dance, dance education, folk dance, modern dance.

Typical Sequence of College Courses: Introduction to music, anatomy and kinesiology for dance, history of dance, dance improvisation, methods of teaching dance, dance composition, dance notation, dance technique (e.g., ballet, tap, modern). **Typical Sequence of High School Courses:** Biology, foreign language, dance, music.

Career Snapshot: Dance is one of the most basic arts of all because the medium is the dancer's own body. This means that dance is also a physical discipline as demanding as any sport. Most dancers start training at a very early age and often must give up performing as their bodies age. However, many find continuing satisfaction and employment in dance instruction and choreography. This is a very competitive field, and only the most talented find regular employment as dancers or choreographers. Job opportunities are better for dance teachers.

Related Jobs			
Job Title	Average Earnings	Job Growth	Job Openings
1. Art, Drama, and Music Teachers, Postsecondary	$49,740	32.2%	329,000
2. Choreographers	$34,720	16.8%	4,000
3. Dancers	No data available	16.8%	4,000
Job 1 shares 329,000 job openings with 35 jobs not included in the list.			

© JIST Works

Characteristics of the Related Jobs: Interests—Artistic; Social; Investigative. **Skills**—Instructing; social perceptiveness; persuasion; learning strategies; active listening. **Values**—Creativity; authority; ability utilization; social service; achievement. **Work Conditions**—Indoors, environmentally controlled; spend time keeping or regaining balance; spend time making repetitive motions; extremely bright or inadequate lighting; walking and running.

Dentistry

Prepares individuals for the independent professional practice of dentistry/dental medicine, encompassing the evaluation, diagnosis, prevention, and treatment of diseases, disorders, and conditions of the oral cavity, maxillofacial area, and adjacent structures and their impact on the human body and health. **Related CIP Program:** 51.0401 Dentistry (DDS, DMD).

Specializations in the Major: Endodontics, oral and maxillofacial surgery, oral pathology, orthodontics, periodontics, public health dentistry.

Typical Sequence of College Courses: English composition, introduction to psychology, college algebra, introduction to business management, introduction to sociology, oral communication, general chemistry, general biology, organic chemistry, nutrition, introduction to accounting, introduction to biochemistry, dental morphology and function, occlusion, dental materials, ethics in health care, head and neck anatomy, oral radiology, assessment and treatment planning, dental anesthesia, pharmacology, prosthodontics (fixed/removable, partial/complete), community dentistry programs, endodontics, oral pathology, pediatric dentistry, dental emergency diagnosis and treatment, chronic orofacial pain, oral implantology, professional practice management, clinical experience in dentistry. **Typical Sequence of High School Courses:** English, algebra, geometry, trigonometry, biology, computer science, public speaking, chemistry, foreign language, physics, pre-calculus.

Career Snapshot: Dentists generally get at least eight years of education beyond high school. Those who want to teach or do research usually must get additional education. Besides academic ability, students of dentistry need good eye-hand coordination and communication skills. Although it seems unlikely that a vaccine against decay germs will be developed anytime soon, tooth sealants and fluoridation have reduced the incidence of tooth decay among young people, which means that dentistry's emphasis has shifted to prevention and maintenance. Note that as long as you take the courses that dentistry schools require for admissions, you have quite a lot of choice about your undergraduate major.

Related Jobs			
Job Title	Average Earnings	Job Growth	Job Openings
1. Dentists, General	$122,430	13.5%	7,000
2. Health Specialties Teachers, Postsecondary	$70,310	32.2%	329,000

Job 2 shares 329,000 job openings with 35 jobs not included in the list.

Characteristics of the Related Jobs: Interests—Investigative; Social; Realistic. **Skills**—Science; instructing; complex problem solving; reading comprehension; critical thinking. **Values**—Social service; authority; social status; responsibility; achievement. **Work Conditions**—Exposed to disease or infections; exposed to radiation; sitting; indoors, environmentally controlled; hazardous conditions.

Dietetics

Prepares individuals to integrate and apply the principles of the food and nutrition sciences, human behavior, and the biomedical sciences to design and manage effective nutrition programs in a variety of settings. **Related CIP Programs:** 51.3102 Clinical Nutrition/Nutritionist; 51.3101 Dietetics/Dietitian (R.D.).

Specializations in the Major: Clinical dietetics, community dietetics, dietetics education, food service management, research dietetics.

Typical Sequence of College Courses: English composition, college algebra, general biology, general chemistry, organic chemistry, oral communication, statistics, introduction to computer science, microbiology, introduction to economics, introduction to business management, introduction to biochemistry, introduction to food science and technology, human anatomy, human physiology, nutrition through life, food service operational management, diet therapy, menu management, community nutrition. **Typical Sequence of High School Courses:** English, algebra, social science, biology, trigonometry, chemistry, physics, geometry.

© JIST Works

Career Snapshot: Dietitians plan food and nutrition programs and supervise the preparation and serving of food. They are concerned with creating diets that are healthful, appetizing, and within budget. They need to know about human nutritional needs in sickness and health, cultural preferences for foods, the nutritional properties of various foods and how they are affected by preparation techniques, and the business or health care environment in which food is prepared and served. A bachelor's degree is good preparation for entering this field; for research, teaching, advanced management, or public health, a graduate degree is helpful or required. Job opportunities are expected to be good, especially for those who have specialized in nutritional needs of people with kidney or diabetes problems.

Related Jobs			
Job Title	Average Earnings	Job Growth	Job Openings
1. Dietetic Technicians	$23,350	19.1%	3,000
2. Dietitians and Nutritionists	$44,370	18.3%	4,000

Characteristics of the Related Jobs: Interests—Investigative; Social; Realistic. **Skills**—Social perceptiveness; instructing; service orientation; learning strategies; active learning. **Values**—Social service; authority; ability utilization; co-workers; creativity. **Work Conditions**—Exposed to disease or infections; minor burns, cuts, bites, or stings; common protective or safety equipment; walking and running; standing.

Drama/Theater Arts

Focuses on the general study of dramatic works and their performance. **Related CIP Program:** 50.0501 Drama and Dramatics/Theatre Arts, General.

Specializations in the Major: Acting, design and technology, directing.

Typical Sequence of College Courses: English composition, foreign language, history of theater, acting technique, dramatic literature, performance techniques, theater technology (e.g., set/costume/lighting), theater practicum. **Typical Sequence of High School Courses:** English, foreign language, literature, public speaking.

Career Snapshot: Drama is one of the most ancient art forms and continues to entertain audiences today. As in all performing arts, there are better opportunities for teachers than for performers. Teaching at the postsecondary level usually requires a master's degree. The technical aspects of theater—set design, lighting, costume design, and makeup—also offer jobs for nonperformers. The academic program includes many opportunities to learn through student performances.

Related Jobs			
Job Title	Average Earnings	Job Growth	Job Openings
1. Actors	No data available	16.1%	11,000
2. Art, Drama, and Music Teachers, Postsecondary	$49,740	32.2%	329,000
3. Directors—Stage, Motion Pictures, Television, and Radio	$52,440	16.6%	11,000
4. Producers	$52,440	16.6%	11,000
5. Program Directors	$52,440	16.6%	11,000
6. Talent Directors	$52,440	16.6%	11,000
7. Technical Directors/ Managers	$52,440	16.6%	11,000

Job 1 shares 329,000 job openings with 35 jobs not included in the list. Jobs 2, 3, 4, 5, and 6 share 11,000 job openings.

Characteristics of the Related Jobs: Interests—Artistic; Enterprising; Social. **Skills**—Management of personnel resources; speaking; social perceptiveness; time management; active listening. **Values**—Creativity; authority; ability utilization; recognition; autonomy. **Work Conditions**—Indoors, environmentally controlled; sitting.

Early Childhood Education

Prepares individuals to teach students in formal settings prior to beginning regular elementary school, usually ranging in age from three to six years (or grade one), depending on the school system or state regulations; includes preparation to teach all relevant subject matter. **Related CIP Programs:** 13.1210 Early Childhood Education and Teaching; 13.1209 Kindergarten/ Preschool Education and Teaching.

Specializations in the Major: Art education, bilingual education, music education, reading readiness.

Typical Sequence of College Courses: Introduction to psychology, English composition, oral communication, history and philosophy of education, human growth and development, teaching methods, educational alternatives for exceptional students, educational psychology, reading assessment and teaching, mathematics education, art education, music education, physical education, health education, science education, children's literature, student teaching. **Typical Sequence of High School Courses:** English, algebra, geometry, trigonometry, science, foreign language, public speaking.

Career Snapshot: Because very young children do not think exactly the same way as we do, an important part of an early childhood education major is learning effective educational techniques for this age group. As in any other teaching major, a bachelor's degree is the minimum requirement for employment, and a master's degree is often needed for job security and a pay raise. Although enrollments of very young students are expected to decline for some time, jobs will open to replace teachers who are retiring. Best opportunities are expected in high-growth regions of the country and in inner-city and rural schools.

Related Jobs			
Job Title	Average Earnings	Job Growth	Job Openings
1. Kindergarten Teachers, Except Special Education	$42,050	22.4%	28,000
2. Preschool Teachers, Except Special Education	$21,550	33.1%	77,000

Characteristics of the Related Jobs: Interests—Social; Artistic; Investigative. **Skills**—Learning strategies; social perceptiveness; instructing; negotiation; monitoring. **Values**—Social service; authority; creativity; responsibility; achievement. **Work Conditions**—Exposed to disease or infections; spend time kneeling, crouching, stooping, or crawling; spend time bending or twisting the body; walking and running; standing.

Economics

Focuses on the systematic study of the production, conservation, and allocation of resources in conditions of scarcity, together with the organizational frameworks related to these processes. **Related CIP Program:** 45.0601 Economics, General.

Specializations in the Major: Applied economics, econometrics, economic theory.

Typical Sequence of College Courses: English composition, introduction to psychology, introduction to sociology, American government, foreign language, statistics, calculus, introduction to economics, statistics for business and social sciences, introduction to computer science, microeconomic theory, macroeconomic theory, mathematical methods in economics, econometrics. **Typical Sequence of High School Courses:** Algebra, English, foreign language, social science, trigonometry, pre-calculus.

Career Snapshot: Economics is most basically the study of human needs and how they are satisfied. Therefore, it looks at how goods and services are produced, distributed, and consumed; how markets for these goods and services are created and behave; and how the actions of individuals, businesses, and governments affect these markets. Graduates of economics programs may work for business, government, or universities. With teacher training, some may find jobs in secondary schools, where economics is becoming a popular course. The best job opportunities should be in the private sector for those with graduate degrees.

Related Jobs			
Job Title	**Average Earnings**	**Job Growth**	**Job Openings**
1. Economics Teachers, Postsecondary	$68,050	32.2%	329,000
2. Economists	$72,370	5.6%	1,000
3. Market Research Analysts	$57,150	19.6%	20,000
4. Survey Researchers	$27,900	25.9%	3,000

Job 1 shares 329,000 job openings with 35 jobs not included in the list.

Characteristics of the Related Jobs: Interests—Investigative; Enterprising; Conventional. **Skills**—Persuasion; negotiation; writing; time management;

© JIST Works

coordination. **Values**—Autonomy; working conditions; recognition; creativity; advancement. **Work Conditions**—Sitting; indoors, environmentally controlled.

Electrical Engineering

Prepares individuals to apply mathematical and scientific principles to the design, development, and operational evaluation of electrical, electronic, and related communications systems and their components, including electrical power generation systems; and the analysis of problems such as superconductor, wave propagation, energy storage and retrieval, and reception and amplification. **Related CIP Program:** 14.1001 Electrical, Electronics, and Communications Engineering.

Specializations in the Major: Aerospace applications, broadcasting, communications, computers, controls, power generation/transmission.

Typical Sequence of College Courses: English composition, technical writing, calculus, differential equations, introduction to computer science, general chemistry, general physics, introduction to engineering, introduction to electric circuits, engineering circuit analysis, signals and systems, semiconductor devices, digital systems, logic design, electromagnetic fields, communication systems, control systems, senior design project. **Typical Sequence of High School Courses:** English, algebra, geometry, trigonometry, pre-calculus, calculus, chemistry, physics, computer science.

Career Snapshot: Electrical engineers apply principles of physics, chemistry, and materials science to the generation, transmission, and use of electric power. They may develop huge dynamos or tiny chips. Usually they enter the field with a bachelor's degree. Management may be an option later in their careers. Electricity is not likely to be replaced as a power source anytime soon, and new electronic devices are being developed constantly, so the job outlook for electrical engineers is expected to be good despite foreign competition.

Related Jobs			
Job Title	*Average Earnings*	*Job Growth*	*Job Openings*
1. Electrical Engineers	$72,770	11.8%	12,000
2. Electronics Engineers, Except Computer	$76,810	9.7%	11,000

(continued)

(continued)

Job Title	Average Earnings	Job Growth	Job Openings
3. Engineering Managers	$99,000	13.0%	15,000
4. Engineering Teachers, Postsecondary	$74,840	32.2%	329,000

Job 4 shares 329,000 job openings with 35 jobs not included in the list.

Characteristics of the Related Jobs: Interests—Investigative; Realistic; Enterprising. **Skills**—Technology design; science; operations analysis; troubleshooting; management of financial resources. **Values**—Creativity; authority; ability utilization; autonomy; social status. **Work Conditions**—Sitting; indoors, environmentally controlled; noise levels are distracting or uncomfortable; common protective or safety equipment; hazardous conditions.

Elementary Education

Prepares individuals to teach students in the elementary grades, which may include kindergarten through grade eight, depending on the school system or state regulations; includes preparation to teach all elementary education subject matter. **Related CIP Program:** 13.1202 Elementary Education and Teaching.

Specializations in the Major: Art education, bilingual education, mathematics education, music education, reading, science education.

Typical Sequence of College Courses: Introduction to psychology, English composition, oral communication, history and philosophy of education, human growth and development, teaching methods, educational alternatives for exceptional students, educational psychology, reading assessment and teaching, mathematics education, art education, physical education, social studies education, health education, science education, language arts and literature, student teaching. **Typical Sequence of High School Courses:** English, algebra, geometry, trigonometry, science, foreign language, public speaking.

Career Snapshot: In elementary education it is usually possible to specialize in a particular subject, such as reading or science, or to get a general background. Everyone in this field needs to learn general principles of how young people develop physically and mentally, as well as the teaching and

© JIST Works

classroom-management techniques that work best with children of this age. A bachelor's degree is often sufficient to enter this career, but in many school districts it is expected that you will continue your education as far as a master's degree. Enrollments in elementary schools are expected to decline for some time, but there will be job growth in Sunbelt communities and many openings to replace teachers who retire.

Job Title	Related Job		
	Average Earnings	Job Growth	Job Openings
Elementary School Teachers, Except Special Education	$43,660	18.2%	203,000

Characteristics of the Related Job: Interest—Social. **Skills**—Instructing; learning strategies; social perceptiveness; monitoring; persuasion. **Values**—Authority; social service; creativity; responsibility; achievement. **Work Conditions**—Exposed to disease or infections; standing; noise levels are distracting or uncomfortable; walking and running; spend time kneeling, crouching, stooping, or crawling.

English

Focuses on the English language, including its history, structure and related communications skills; and the literature and culture of English-speaking peoples. **Related CIP Program:** 23.0101 English Language and Literature, General.

Specializations in the Major: Creative writing, English education, language, literature.

Typical Sequence of College Courses: English composition, introduction to literary study, foreign language, survey of British literature, survey of American literature, a major writer (e.g., Shakespeare, Romantic poets), a genre (e.g., drama, short story, poetry), creative writing, history of the English language, comparative literature. **Typical Sequence of High School Courses:** English, foreign language, literature, history, public speaking, social science.

Career Snapshot: English majors not only learn about a great literary tradition, but they also develop first-rate writing and critical-thinking skills that can be valuable in a variety of careers. Besides teaching, many of them go into business, law, and library science, usually with an appropriate master's or law degree. They are said to make excellent trainees in computer programming. In a wide range of careers, their humanistic skills often allow them to advance higher than those who prepare through more specifically career-oriented curricula.

	Related Job		
Job Title	Average Earnings	Job Growth	Job Openings
English Language and Literature Teachers, Postsecondary	$48,920	32.2%	329,000

This job shares 329,000 job openings with 35 jobs not included in the list.

Characteristics of the Related Job: Interests—Artistic; Social; Investigative. **Skills**—Instructing; learning strategies; social perceptiveness; persuasion; writing. **Values**—Authority; social service; creativity; achievement; ability utilization. **Work Conditions**—Indoors, environmentally controlled; sitting.

Environmental Science

Focuses on the application of biological, chemical, and physical principles to the study of the physical environment and the solution of environmental problems, including subjects such as abating or controlling environmental pollution and degradation; the interaction between human society and the natural environment; and natural resources management. **Related CIP Programs:** 03.0104 Environmental Science; 03.0103 Environmental Studies.

Specializations in the Major: Environmental education, environmental policy, environmental technology, land resources, natural history.

Typical Sequence of College Courses: English composition, college algebra, general biology, general chemistry, organic chemistry, oral communication, statistics, introduction to computer science, introduction to geology, ecology, introduction to environmental science, natural resource

© JIST Works

management and water quality, microbiology, introduction to economics, introduction to ground water/hydrology, regional planning and environmental protection, environmental impact assessment, environmental economics, environmental law, environmental chemistry. **Typical Sequence of High School Courses:** Biology, chemistry, algebra, geometry, trigonometry, computer science, English, public speaking, geography.

Career Snapshot: Environmental science (or studies) is a multidisciplinary subject that involves a number of sciences such as biology, geology, and chemistry, as well as social sciences such as economics and geography. It also touches on urban/regional planning and on law and public policy. Those with a bachelor's degree may work for an environmental consulting business or a government planning agency, or may go on to get a graduate or professional degree in one of these related fields.

Related Jobs			
Job Title	Average Earnings	Job Growth	Job Openings
1. Environmental Science and Protection Technicians, Including Health	$35,480	16.3%	6,000
2. Environmental Science Teachers, Postsecondary	$61,490	32.2%	329,000
3. Environmental Scientists and Specialists, Including Health	$51,950	17.1%	8,000

Job 2 shares 329,000 job openings with 35 jobs not included in the list.

Characteristics of the Related Jobs: Interests—Investigative; Realistic. **Skills**—Science; persuasion; negotiation; service orientation; coordination. **Values**—Creativity; autonomy; ability utilization; recognition; responsibility. **Work Conditions**—Outdoors, exposed to weather; very hot or cold; extremely bright or inadequate lighting; contaminants; noise levels are distracting or uncomfortable.

Family and Consumer Sciences

Focuses on how individuals develop and function in family, work, and community settings and how they relate to their physical, social, emotional, and intellectual environments. **Related CIP Programs:** 19.0201 Business Family and Consumer Sciences/Human Sciences; 19.0402 Consumer Economics; 19.0203 Consumer Merchandising/Retailing Management; 19.0403 Consumer Services and Advocacy; 13.1308 Family and Consumer Sciences/Home Economics Teacher Education; 19.0202 Family and Consumer Sciences/Human Sciences Communication; 19.0101 Family and Consumer Sciences/Human Sciences, General; 19.0401 Family Resource Management Studies, General.

Specializations in the Major: Child care and family life, clothing and textiles, consumer merchandising, consumer services and advocacy, family financial management, foods and nutrition, human sciences communication.

Typical Sequence of College Courses: Introduction to psychology, English composition, oral communication, history and philosophy of education, human growth and development, foods, textiles, introduction to nutrition, introduction to interior design, marriage and the family, consumer economics, housing, clothing and fashion, student teaching. **Typical Sequence of High School Courses:** English, algebra, geometry, trigonometry, science, foreign language, home economics, public speaking.

Career Snapshot: Family and consumer sciences, which used to be called home economics, is a combination of several concerns related to families and their economic needs and behaviors. Some programs are designed to prepare home economics educators and, therefore, include courses on teaching strategies and classroom management, plus student teaching. Some graduates work in industries that market to families. Some become financial advisors. Others pursue a higher degree with the goal of working for the federal government as a cooperative extension agent.

Related Jobs			
Job Title	Average Earnings	Job Growth	Job Openings
1. Creative Writers	$45,460	17.7%	14,000
2. Education Teachers, Postsecondary	$50,410	32.2%	329,000

© JIST Works

3. Farm and Home Management Advisors	$41,270	7.7%	2,000
4. First-Line Supervisors/ Managers of Retail Sales Workers	$32,410	3.8%	229,000
5. Home Economics Teachers, Postsecondary	$47,670	32.2%	329,000
6. Marketing Managers	$90,450	20.8%	23,000
7. Middle School Teachers, Except Special and Vocational Education	$44,180	13.7%	83,000
8. Public Relations Specialists	$44,390	22.9%	38,000
9. Sales Managers	$85,980	19.7%	40,000
10. Secondary School Teachers, Except Special and Vocational Education	$46,120	14.4%	107,000

Job 1 shares 14,000 job openings with 3 jobs not included in the list. Jobs 2 and 5 share 329,000 job openings with each other and with 34 jobs not included in the list.

Characteristics of the Related Jobs: Interests—Social; Enterprising; Conventional. **Skills**—Persuasion; instructing; social perceptiveness; monitoring; learning strategies. **Values**—Authority; creativity; social service; responsibility; autonomy. **Work Conditions**—Walking and running; standing; indoors, environmentally controlled; exposed to disease or infections.

Film/Cinema Studies

Film/Cinema Studies focuses on the study of the history, development, theory, and criticism of the film/video arts, as well as the basic principles of film making and film production. **Related CIP Programs:** 50.0602 Cinematography and Film/Video Production; 50.0601 Film/Cinema Studies.

Specializations in the Major: Criticism, directing/producing, editing, screenwriting.

Typical Sequence of College Courses: English composition, foreign language, world history in the modern era, introduction to psychology, film as a narrative art, history of film, film styles and genres, major film directors, literature and media, film theory and criticism, gender and film, seminar (reporting on research). **Typical Sequence of High School Courses:** English, foreign language, literature, history, photography.

Career Snapshot: Film is one of the newest art forms and still straddles the borderline between popular culture and high art. The American film and video industry continues to grow as it increasingly dominates the world market, but there is keen competition for creative jobs in this field. Some graduates of film programs become critics or work in industrial or educational film production. Students can usually tailor the academic program to emphasize the aspect of film that interests them; therefore, they may do a lot of writing about film or hands-on work producing film.

Related Jobs			
Job Title	*Average Earnings*	*Job Growth*	*Job Openings*
1. Art, Drama, and Music Teachers, Postsecondary	$49,740	32.2%	329,000
2. Camera Operators, Television, Video, and Motion Picture	$38,900	14.2%	4,000
3. Directors—Stage, Motion Pictures, Television, and Radio	$52,440	16.6%	11,000
4. Film and Video Editors	$44,750	18.6%	3,000
5. Producers	$52,440	16.6%	11,000
6. Program Directors	$52,440	16.6%	11,000
7. Talent Directors	$52,440	16.6%	11,000
8. Technical Directors/ Managers	$52,440	16.6%	11,000

Job 1 shares 329,000 job openings with 35 jobs not included in the list. Jobs 3, 5, 6, 7, and 8 share 11,000 job openings.

Characteristics of the Related Jobs: Interests—Artistic; Enterprising; Social. **Skills**—Management of personnel resources; time management; speaking; coordination; persuasion. **Values**—Authority; creativity; responsibility; autonomy; ability utilization. **Work Conditions**—Indoors, environmentally controlled; sitting.

© JIST Works

Finance

Prepares individuals to plan, manage, and analyze the financial and monetary aspects and performance of business enterprises, banking institutions, or other organizations. **Related CIP Program:** 52.0801 Finance, General.

Specializations in the Major: Corporate finance, public finance, securities analysis.

Typical Sequence of College Courses: English composition, business writing, introduction to psychology, principles of microeconomics, principles of macroeconomics, calculus for business and social sciences, statistics for business and social sciences, introduction to management information systems, introduction to accounting, legal environment of business, principles of management and organization, operations management, strategic management, business finance, introduction to marketing, corporate finance, money and capital markets, investment analysis. **Typical Sequence of High School Courses:** English, algebra, geometry, trigonometry, science, foreign language, computer science.

Career Snapshot: Finance is the study of how organizations acquire funds and use them in ways that maximize their value. The banking and insurance industries, as well as investment service companies, employ graduates of this field. A bachelor's degree is good preparation for entry-level jobs.

Related Jobs			
Job Title	Average Earnings	Job Growth	Job Openings
1. Budget Analysts	$57,190	13.5%	6,000
2. Business Teachers, Postsecondary	$58,230	32.2%	329,000
3. Credit Analysts	$48,800	3.6%	3,000
4. Financial Analysts	$62,780	17.3%	28,000
5. Financial Managers, Branch or Department	$83,780	14.8%	63,000
6. Loan Officers	$49,180	8.3%	38,000
7. Personal Financial Advisors	$62,450	25.9%	17,000

(continued)

(continued)

Job Title	Average Earnings	Job Growth	Job Openings
8. Treasurers, Controllers, and Chief Financial Officers	$83,780	14.8%	63,000

Job 2 shares 329,000 job openings with 35 jobs not included in the list.

Characteristics of the Related Jobs: Interests—Enterprising; Conventional; Social. **Skills**—Management of financial resources; judgment and decision making; systems evaluation; complex problem solving; systems analysis. **Values**—Authority; working conditions; advancement; autonomy; responsibility. **Work Conditions**—Sitting; indoors, environmentally controlled.

Food Science

Focuses on the application of biological, chemical, and physical principles to the study of converting raw agricultural products into processed forms suitable for direct human consumption, and the storage of such products. **Related CIP Programs:** 01.1001 Food Science; 01.1002 Food Technology and Processing.

Specializations in the Major: Food quality assurance, food research, management of food processing, product development.

Typical Sequence of College Courses: English composition, college algebra, general biology, general chemistry, organic chemistry, oral communication, statistics, introduction to computer science, microbiology, introduction to economics, general physics, introduction to biochemistry, introduction to food science and technology, food chemistry, food analysis, food processing, food bacteriology, nutrition, food plant engineering. **Typical Sequence of High School Courses:** Biology, chemistry, algebra, geometry, trigonometry, computer science, English, public speaking.

Career Snapshot: A glance at the label on a package of food will tell you that the science of making, packaging, and ensuring the quality of foods involves both biology and chemistry. Food science graduates work in research, product development, and quality control. A bachelor's degree is usually sufficient for an entry-level job in quality control. But for advancement and for research jobs, a graduate degree is a help.

© JIST Works

Related Jobs			
Job Title	Average Earnings	Job Growth	Job Openings
1. Agricultural Sciences Teachers, Postsecondary	$70,610	32.2%	329,000
2. Agricultural Technicians	$30,630	13.4%	1,000
3. Chemical Technicians	$38,620	4.4%	7,000
4. Food Science Technicians	$30,630	13.4%	1,000
5. Food Scientists and Technologists	$51,320	10.9%	1,000

Job 1 shares 329,000 job openings with 35 jobs not included in the list. Jobs 2 and 4 share 1,000 job openings.

Characteristics of the Related Jobs: Interests—Realistic; Investigative; Conventional. **Skills**—Science; operation monitoring; quality control analysis; equipment maintenance; troubleshooting. **Values**—Variety; advancement; working conditions; creativity; security. **Work Conditions**—Common protective or safety equipment; hazardous conditions; contaminants; noise levels are distracting or uncomfortable; indoors, environmentally controlled.

Forestry

Prepares individuals to manage and develop forest areas for economic, recreational, and ecological purposes. **Related CIP Program:** 03.0501 Forestry, General.

Specializations in the Major: Forest management, forest product production, forest restoration, urban forestry.

Typical Sequence of College Courses: English composition, calculus, general biology, general chemistry, organic chemistry, introduction to geology, oral communication, statistics, computer applications in agriculture, introduction to soil science, ecology, introduction to forestry, dendrology, forest ecology, silviculture, forest resources policy, forest inventory and growth, forest surveying and mapping, tree pests and diseases, wood properties and utilization, forest economics and valuation, forest watershed management, timber harvesting, introduction to wildlife conservation, remote sensing.

Typical Sequence of High School Courses: Biology, chemistry, algebra, geometry, trigonometry, computer science, English, public speaking, geography.

Career Snapshot: Foresters manage wooded land. Most of them work for governments and are concerned with conservation and fire prevention. Some work for logging companies and plan how to harvest timber economically, safely, and in keeping with environmental laws. Foresters also help plant and grow trees to regenerate forests. A bachelor's degree is usually a good preparation for this field, and the job outlook is good because of increasing interest in preserving the environment and, at the same time, the opening of some public lands to timber harvesting.

	Related Jobs		
Job Title	Average Earnings	Job Growth	Job Openings
1. Forest and Conservation Technicians	$33,250	6.6%	6,000
2. Forest and Conservation Workers	$19,940	6.0%	2,000
3. Foresters	$48,800	6.7%	1,000
4. Park Naturalists	$52,330	6.3%	2,000
5. Range Managers	$52,330	6.3%	2,000
6. Soil Conservationists	$52,330	6.3%	2,000

Jobs 4, 5, and 6 share 2,000 job openings.

Characteristics of the Related Jobs: Interests—Realistic; Investigative. **Skills**—Science; management of financial resources; persuasion; management of personnel resources; coordination. **Values**—Autonomy; creativity; responsibility; ability utilization; independence. **Work Conditions**—Outdoors, exposed to weather; very hot or cold; minor burns, cuts, bites, or stings; common protective or safety equipment; extremely bright or inadequate lighting.

French

Focuses on the French language and related dialects and creoles; includes the cultural and historical contexts and applications to business, science/technology, and other settings. **Related CIP Program:** 16.0901 French Language and Literature.

Specializations in the Major: History and culture, language education, literature, translation.

© JIST Works

Typical Sequence of College Courses: French language, conversation, composition, linguistics, French literature, French history and civilization, European history and civilization, grammar, phonetics. **Typical Sequence of High School Courses:** English, public speaking, French, history, literature, social science.

Career Snapshot: French is a native tongue on several continents and in parts of the United States, and it has a rich cultural heritage associated with the arts and literature. French majors may go into careers in international business, travel, or teaching. Teaching at the secondary level requires education courses and, in many districts, a master's; college teaching requires a graduate degree.

	Related Jobs		
Job Title	Average Earnings	Job Growth	Job Openings
1. Foreign Language and Literature Teachers, Postsecondary	$49,120	32.2%	329,000
2. Interpreters and Translators	$34,900	19.9%	4,000

Job 1 shares 329,000 job openings with 35 jobs not included in the list.

Characteristics of the Related Jobs: Interests—Artistic; Social; Investigative. **Skills**—Writing; active listening; speaking; reading comprehension; service orientation. **Values**—Social service; ability utilization; achievement; autonomy; social status. **Work Conditions**—Sitting; indoors, environmentally controlled.

Geography

Focuses on the systematic study of the spatial distribution and interrelationships of people, natural resources, plant and animal life. **Related CIP Program:** 45.0701 Geography.

Specializations in the Major: Development, environmental science, geographic information systems, management and policy, urban planning.

Typical Sequence of College Courses: English composition, American history, foreign language, introduction to economics, introduction to sociology, statistics, introduction to computer science, introduction to geology, introduction to human geography, economic geography, world history in the modern era, thematic cartography, geography of a region, physical geography, field geography, research techniques in geography, quantitative methods in geography, remote sensing, geographic information systems (GIS). **Typical Sequence of High School Courses:** Art, English, social science, foreign language, trigonometry, history, geography, computer science.

Career Snapshot: Geography studies how people and their environments relate to one another. It analyzes the human habitat spatially and records information about it in various forms, with an increasing emphasis on databases. Geographers work for governments, public-interest organizations, and businesses. They help with site planning, environmental impact studies, market research, competitive intelligence, and military intelligence. Best job opportunities will be for those who know how to use geographic information system (GIS) technology.

Related Jobs			
Job Title	Average Earnings	Job Growth	Job Openings
1. Geographers	$61,520	6.8%	fewer than 500
2. Geography Teachers, Postsecondary	$57,370	32.2%	329,000

Job 2 shares 329,000 job openings with 35 jobs not included in the list.

Characteristics of the Related Jobs: Interests—Investigative; Realistic; Conventional. **Skills**—Instructing; writing; learning strategies; science; critical thinking. **Values**—Autonomy; creativity; ability utilization; responsibility; social status. **Work Conditions**—Indoors, environmentally controlled; sitting.

Geology

Focuses on the scientific study of the earth; the forces acting upon it; and the behavior of the solids, liquids and gases comprising it. **Related CIP Program:** 40.0601 Geology/Earth Science, General.

Specializations in the Major: Engineering geology, geophysics, mineralogy, oceanography, paleontology, petroleum geology, stratigraphy, volcanology.

Typical Sequence of College Courses: English composition, calculus, introduction to computer science, general chemistry, general physics, introduction to geology, invertebrate paleontology, summer field geology, structural geology, mineralogy, optical mineralogy, igneous and metamorphic petrology, sedimentary petrology, stratigraphy. **Typical Sequence of High School Courses:** English, algebra, geometry, trigonometry, chemistry, physics, pre-calculus, computer science, calculus.

Career Snapshot: Geology is the study of the physical makeup, processes, and history of the earth. Geologists use knowledge of this field to locate water, mineral, and petroleum resources; to protect the environment; and to offer advice on construction and land-use projects. A bachelor's degree opens the door for many entry-level jobs, but a master's degree helps for advancement and is thought to be the degree that now leads to the best opportunities. Many research jobs in universities and the government require a Ph.D. Some field research requires going to remote places, but it is also possible to specialize in laboratory sciences.

Related Jobs			
Job Title	*Average Earnings*	*Job Growth*	*Job Openings*
1. Atmospheric, Earth, Marine, and Space Sciences Teachers, Postsecondary	$65,250	32.2%	329,000
2. Geologists	$70,180	8.3%	2,000
3. Geoscientists, Except Hydrologists and Geographers	$70,180	8.3%	2,000
4. Hydrologists	$60,880	31.6%	1,000
5. Natural Sciences Managers	$90,080	13.6%	5,000

Job 1 shares 329,000 job openings with 35 jobs not included in the list.

Characteristics of the Related Jobs: Interests—Investigative; Realistic; Enterprising. **Skills**—Science; active learning; mathematics; critical thinking; writing. **Values**—Creativity; responsibility; autonomy; ability utilization; authority. **Work Conditions**—Sitting; hazardous conditions; indoors, environmentally controlled; outdoors, exposed to weather.

Geophysics

Focuses on the scientific study of the physics of solids and its application to the study of the earth and other planets. **Related CIP Program:** 40.0603 Geophysics and Seismology.

Specializations in the Major: Atmospheric physics, environmental geophysics, geomagnetism, paleomagnetism, physical oceanography, remote sensing, seismology, volcanology.

Typical Sequence of College Courses: English composition, calculus, introduction to computer science, general chemistry, general physics, introduction to geology, summer field geology, structural geology, mineralogy, remote sensing, exploration geophysics, physical oceanography, stratigraphy, igneous and metamorphic petrology. **Typical Sequence of High School Courses:** English, algebra, geometry, trigonometry, chemistry, physics, precalculus, computer science, calculus.

Career Snapshot: Geophysics uses physical measurements and mathematical models to describe the structure, composition, and processes of the earth and planets. Geophysicists study seismic waves and variations in gravitation and terrestrial magnetism, thus learning where petroleum and minerals are deposited, where (and sometimes even when) earthquakes and volcanic eruptions are likely to strike, and how to solve environmental problems such as pollution. A bachelor's degree can lead to entry-level jobs, but a higher degree opens greater potential for advancement in research, as well as opportunities in college teaching.

Related Jobs			
Job Title	Average Earnings	Job Growth	Job Openings
1. Atmospheric, Earth, Marine, and Space Sciences Teachers, Postsecondary	$65,250	32.2%	329,000
2. Geologists	$70,180	8.3%	2,000

© JIST Works

3. Geoscientists, Except Hydrologists and Geographers	$70,180	8.3%	2,000
4. Natural Sciences Managers	$90,080	13.6%	5,000

Job 1 shares 329,000 job openings with 35 jobs not included in the list.

Characteristics of the Related Jobs: Interests—Investigative; Realistic; Enterprising. **Skills**—Science; active learning; management of financial resources; time management; mathematics. **Values**—Creativity; responsibility; autonomy; authority; ability utilization. **Work Conditions**—Hazardous conditions; sitting; indoors, environmentally controlled; noise levels are distracting or uncomfortable; outdoors, exposed to weather.

German

Focuses on the German language and related dialects as used in Austria, Germany, Switzerland, neighboring European countries containing German-speaking minorities, and elsewhere; includes the cultural and historical contexts and applications to business, science/technology, and other settings. **Related CIP Program:** 16.0501 German Language and Literature.

Specializations in the Major: History and culture, language education, literature, translation.

Typical Sequence of College Courses: German language, conversation, composition, linguistics, German literature, German history and civilization, European history and civilization, grammar, phonetics. **Typical Sequence of High School Courses:** English, public speaking, German, history, literature, social science.

Career Snapshot: United once again, Germany is a major economic and cultural force in Europe and the world. A degree in German can open many doors in international business, travel, and law. Many employers are looking for graduates with an understanding of a second language and culture. Those with a graduate degree in German may go into translation or college teaching. With coursework in education, high school teaching is an option; many districts require a master's.

Related Jobs			
Job Title	Average Earnings	Job Growth	Job Openings
1. Foreign Language and Literature Teachers, Postsecondary	$49,120	32.2%	329,000
2. Interpreters and Translators	$34,900	19.9%	4,000

Job 1 shares 329,000 job openings with 35 jobs not included in the list.

Characteristics of the Related Jobs: Interests—Artistic; Social; Investigative. **Skills**—Writing; active listening; speaking; reading comprehension; service orientation. **Values**—Social service; ability utilization; achievement; autonomy; social status. **Work Conditions**—Sitting; indoors, environmentally controlled.

Graphic Design, Commercial Art, and Illustration

Prepares individuals to use artistic techniques to effectively communicate ideas and information to business and consumer audiences via illustrations and other forms of digital or printed media, including documents, images, graphics, sound, and multimedia products on the World Wide Web. **Related CIP Programs:** 50.0402 Commercial and Advertising Art; 11.0801 Web Page, Digital/Multimedia, and Information Resources Design.

Specializations in the Major: Cartooning, illustration, letterform, typography, Web page design.

Typical Sequence of College Courses: English composition, college algebra, basic drawing, oral communication, art history: prehistoric to Renaissance, art history: Renaissance to modern, introduction to graphic design, visual thinking and problem solving, presentation graphics, history of graphic design, letterform, two-dimensional design, three-dimensional design, visual communication, typography, computer applications in graphic design, senior design project. **Typical Sequence of High School Courses:** Algebra, geometry, trigonometry, pre-calculus, English, public speaking, art, computer science, mechanical drawing, photography.

Career Snapshot: Many consumer goods, such as books, magazines, and Web pages, consist primarily of graphic elements—illustrations and text. Other goods, such as cereal boxes, use graphic elements conspicuously. Graphic design teaches you how to represent ideas graphically and give maximum visual appeal to text and pictures. The program involves considerable studio time, and an important goal is creating a good portfolio of work. Graduates with an associate's or bachelor's degree work for publishers and design firms. Some freelance. Competition is expected to be keen; opportunities will be best for those with a bachelor's degree and experience with Web page design or animation.

Related Jobs			
Job Title	Average Earnings	Job Growth	Job Openings
1. Commercial and Industrial Designers	$52,260	10.8%	7,000
2. Computer Programmers	$62,980	2.0%	28,000
3. Graphic Designers	$37,950	15.2%	35,000
4. Multi-Media Artists and Animators	$49,900	14.1%	14,000

Characteristics of the Related Jobs: Interests—Investigative; Realistic; Conventional. **Skills**—Programming; operations analysis; technology design; troubleshooting; complex problem solving. **Values**—Creativity; ability utilization; autonomy; achievement; working conditions. **Work Conditions**—Sitting; spend time making repetitive motions; indoors, environmentally controlled; using hands on objects, tools, or controls.

Health Information Systems Administration

Prepares individuals to plan, design, and manage systems, processes, and facilities used to collect, store, secure, retrieve, analyze, and transmit medical records and other health information used by clinical professionals and health care organizations. **Related CIP Program:** 51.0706 Health Information/Medical Records Administration/Administrator.

Specializations in the Major: Information technology, management.

Typical Sequence of College Courses: English composition, introduction to computer science, college algebra, oral communication, introduction to psychology, accounting, introduction to business management, statistics for business and social sciences, epidemiology, introduction to medical terminology, financial management of health care, human resource management. In health care facilities, legal aspects of health care, American health care systems, introduction to health records, health data and analysis, clinical classification systems, fundamentals of medical science, health data research, seminar (reporting on research). **Typical Sequence of High School Courses:** Algebra, English, geometry, trigonometry, pre-calculus, biology, chemistry, computer science, office computer applications, public speaking, foreign language, social science.

Career Snapshot: Health information systems are needed for much more than billing patients or their HMOs. Many medical discoveries have been made when researchers have examined large collections of health information. Therefore, health information systems administrators must know about the health care system, about various kinds of diseases and vital statistics, about the latest database technologies, and about how researchers compile data to test hypotheses. Some people enter this field with a bachelor's degree, whereas others get a bachelor's degree in another field (perhaps related to health, information systems, or management) and complete a post-graduate certification program.

Related Job			
Job Title	Average Earnings	Job Growth	Job Openings
Medical and Health Services Managers	$68,320	22.8%	33,000

Characteristics of the Related Job: Interests—Enterprising; Social; Investigative. **Skills**—Management of personnel resources; persuasion; service orientation; management of material resources; management of financial resources. **Values**—Authority; social service; creativity; working conditions; social status. **Work Conditions**—Exposed to disease or infections; exposed to radiation; specialized protective or safety equipment; indoors, environmentally controlled; walking and running.

© JIST Works

History

Focuses on the study and interpretation of the past, including the gathering, recording, synthesizing and criticizing of evidence and theories about past events. **Related CIP Programs:** 54.0102 American History (United States); 54.0106 Asian History; 54.0107 Canadian History; 54.0103 European History; 54.0101 History, General; 54.0104 History and Philosophy of Science and Technology; 54.0105 Public/Applied History and Archival Administration.

Specializations in the Major: Applied history, genealogy, history education.

Typical Sequence of College Courses: English composition, foreign language, introduction to philosophy, introduction to political science, world history to the early modern era, world history in the modern era, American history, theory and practice of history, introduction to international relations, seminar (reporting on research). **Typical Sequence of High School Courses:** Algebra, English, foreign language, social science, trigonometry, history.

Career Snapshot: History studies past civilizations in order to understand the present, preserve our heritage, and appreciate the richness of human accomplishment. Almost every field—whether it be in the field of arts, science, or health—includes some study of its past. Therefore, many job opportunities in this field are in teaching. At the secondary level, this requires coursework in education and often a master's. At the postsecondary level, a master's or Ph.D. is necessary. Some historians work as archivists, genealogists, or curators. Some graduates use the critical-thinking skills they develop from history to go into administration or law.

	Related Jobs		
Job Title	Average Earnings	Job Growth	Job Openings
1. Archivists	$37,500	13.4%	1,000
2. Curators	$43,920	15.7%	1,000
3. Historians	$44,950	4.3%	fewer than 500
4. History Teachers, Postsecondary	$54,310	32.2%	329,000
5. Museum Technicians and Conservators	$32,860	14.1%	2,000

Job 4 shares 329,000 job openings with 35 jobs not included in the list.

Characteristics of the Related Jobs: Interests—Investigative; Artistic; Social. **Skills**—Instructing; persuasion; writing; critical thinking; learning strategies. **Values**—Authority; creativity; working conditions; achievement; ability utilization. **Work Conditions**—Sitting.

Hospital/Health Facilities Administration

Prepares individuals to apply managerial principles to the administration of hospitals, clinics, nursing homes, and other health care facilities. **Related CIP Program:** 51.0702 Hospital and Health Care Facilities Administration/Management.

Specializations in the Major: Health policy, hospital management, long-term care management.

Typical Sequence of College Courses: English composition, introduction to economics, college algebra, oral communication, introduction to psychology, accounting, introduction to business management, statistics for business and social sciences, American health care systems, introduction to medical terminology, introduction to management information systems, financial management of health care, human resource mgmt. In health care facilities, strategy and planning for health care, legal aspects of health care, health care and politics. **Typical Sequence of High School Courses:** Algebra, English, geometry, trigonometry, pre-calculus, biology, chemistry, computer science, office computer applications, public speaking, social science, foreign language.

Career Snapshot: Hospital and health facilities administrators need to combine standard business management skills with an understanding of the American health care system and its current issues and trends. They may be generalists who manage an entire facility, or they may specialize in running a department or some specific service of the facility. Generalists are usually expected to have a master's degree, especially in large facilities, whereas specialists or those seeking employment in small facilities may enter with a bachelor's degree. Best employment prospects are in home health agencies and practitioners' offices and clinics, and for those who have experience in a specialized field, such as reimbursement.

© JIST Works

Related Job			
Job Title	Average Earnings	Job Growth	Job Openings
Medical and Health Services Managers	$68,320	22.8%	33,000

Characteristics of the Related Job: Interests—Enterprising; Social; Investigative. **Skills**—Management of personnel resources; persuasion; service orientation; management of material resources; management of financial resources. **Values**—Authority; social service; creativity; working conditions; social status. **Work Conditions**—Exposed to disease or infections; exposed to radiation; specialized protective or safety equipment; indoors, environmentally controlled; walking and running.

Hotel/Motel and Restaurant Management

52.0904 Hotel/Motel Administration/Management prepares individuals to manage operations and facilities that provide lodging services to the traveling public. 52.0906 Resort Management prepares individuals to plan, manage, and market comprehensive vacation facilities and services and related products. 52.0905 Restaurant/Food Services Management prepares individuals to plan, manage, and market restaurants, food services in hospitality establishments, food service chains and franchise networks, and restaurant supply operations. **Related CIP Programs:** 52.0904 Hotel/Motel Administration/Management; 52.0906 Resort Management; 52.0905 Restaurant/Food Services Management.

Specializations in the Major: Hotels/motels, resorts and theme parks, restaurants.

Typical Sequence of College Courses: English composition, business writing, introduction to psychology, principles of microeconomics, principles of macroeconomics, calculus for business and social sciences, statistics for business and social sciences, introduction to management information systems, introduction to accounting, legal environment of business, principles of management and organization, operations management, strategic management, business finance, introduction to marketing, introduction to the hospitality industry, food and beverage production and management, food service and lodging operations, law and the hospitality industry, hotel financial management, marketing hospitality and leisure services, hospitality human resource management, hospitality technology applications, field experience/internship. **Typical Sequence of High School Courses:** English, algebra, geometry, trigonometry, science, foreign language, computer science, public speaking.

Career Snapshot: Students of hotel/motel and restaurant management learn many skills required in any management program—economics, accounting, human resources, finance—plus the specialized skills needed for the hospitality industry. Some enter the field with an associate's degree, but opportunities are better with a bachelor's degree. Usually new hires enter an on-the-job training program where they learn all aspects of the business. The outlook for employment is mostly good, especially in chain restaurants.

Related Jobs			
Job Title	Average Earnings	Job Growth	Job Openings
1. Food Service Managers	$40,600	11.5%	61,000
2. Lodging Managers	$39,100	16.6%	10,000
3. Residential Advisors	$21,770	28.9%	22,000

Characteristics of the Related Jobs: Interests—Enterprising; Social; Conventional. **Skills**—Management of personnel resources; management of financial resources; social perceptiveness; monitoring; time management. **Values**—Authority; creativity; autonomy; responsibility; social service. **Work Conditions**—Walking and running; very hot or cold; minor burns, cuts, bites, or stings; standing; common protective or safety equipment.

Human Resources Management

Prepares individuals to manage the development of human capital in organizations, and to provide related services to individuals and groups. **Related CIP Program:** 52.1001 Human Resources Management/Personnel Administration, General.

Specializations in the Major: Compensation/benefits, job analysis, labor relations, training.

© JIST Works

Typical Sequence of College Courses: English composition, business writing, introduction to psychology, principles of microeconomics, principles of macroeconomics, calculus for business and social sciences, statistics for business and social sciences, introduction to management information systems, introduction to accounting, legal environment of business, principles of management and organization, operations management, strategic management, business finance, introduction to marketing, organizational theory, human resource management, compensation and benefits administration, training and development, employment law, industrial relations and labor management. **Typical Sequence of High School Courses:** English, algebra, geometry, trigonometry, science, foreign language, computer science, public speaking.

Career Snapshot: Human resource managers are responsible for attracting the right employees for an organization, training them, keeping them productively employed, and sometimes severing the relationship through outplacement or retirement. Generalists often enter the field with a bachelor's degree, although specialists may find a master's degree (or perhaps a law degree) advantageous. Generalists most often find entry-level work with small organizations. There is a trend toward outsourcing many specialized functions, such as training and outplacement, to specialized service firms. Specializations that look particularly promising are training, recruiting, and compensation management.

Related Jobs			
Job Title	*Average Earnings*	*Job Growth*	*Job Openings*
1. Business Teachers, Postsecondary	$58,230	32.2%	329,000
2. Compensation and Benefits Managers	$67,040	21.5%	4,000
3. Compensation, Benefits, and Job Analysis Specialists	$48,720	20.4%	15,000
4. Employment Interviewers, Private or Public Employment Service	$41,190	30.5%	30,000
5. Personnel Recruiters	$41,190	30.5%	30,000

(continued)

(continued)

Job Title	Average Earnings	Job Growth	Job Openings
6. Training and Development Managers	$70,430	25.9%	3,000
7. Training and Development Specialists	$45,370	20.8%	32,000

Job 1 shares 329,000 job openings with 35 jobs not included in the list. Jobs 4 and 5 share 30,000 job openings.

Characteristics of the Related Jobs: Interests—Social; Enterprising; Conventional. **Skills**—Persuasion; service orientation; social perceptiveness; instructing; management of personnel resources. **Values**—Social service; working conditions; authority; co-workers; responsibility. **Work Conditions**—Sitting; indoors, environmentally controlled.

Humanities

Focuses on combined studies and research in the humanities subjects as distinguished from the social and physical sciences, emphasizing languages, literatures, art, music, philosophy and religion. **Related CIP Program:** 24.0103 Humanities/Humanistic Studies.

Specializations in the Major: History, language, literature, peace and justice studies, philosophy, religion, the arts.

Typical Sequence of College Courses: Foreign language, major thinkers and issues in philosophy, literature, art and culture, European history and civilization, writing, seminar (reporting on research). **Typical Sequence of High School Courses:** English, algebra, foreign language, history, literature, public speaking, social science.

Career Snapshot: Humanities (sometimes called liberal arts) is an interdisciplinary major that covers a wide range of the arts and other non-scientific modes of thought, such as history, philosophy, religious studies, and language. Graduates of this major usually have strong skills for communicating and critical thinking, and they often advance further in the business world than those who hold more business-focused degrees. Some pursue careers in teaching, media, or the arts. Others get professional degrees in the law or medicine.

© JIST Works

Related Jobs			
Job Title	**Average Earnings**	**Job Growth**	**Job Openings**
1. Anthropology and Archeology Teachers, Postsecondary	$60,190	32.2%	329,000
2. Area, Ethnic, and Cultural Studies Teachers, Postsecondary	$55,660	32.2%	329,000
3. Art, Drama, and Music Teachers, Postsecondary	$49,740	32.2%	329,000
4. Communications Teachers, Postsecondary	$50,610	32.2%	329,000
5. Economics Teachers, Postsecondary	$68,050	32.2%	329,000
6. Education Teachers, Postsecondary	$50,410	32.2%	329,000
7. English Language and Literature Teachers, Postsecondary	$48,920	32.2%	329,000
8. Foreign Language and Literature Teachers, Postsecondary	$49,120	32.2%	329,000
9. Geography Teachers, Postsecondary	$57,370	32.2%	329,000
10. Graduate Teaching Assistants	$27,100	32.2%	329,000

These 10 jobs share 329,000 job openings with each other and with 26 jobs not included in the list.

Characteristics of the Related Jobs: Interests—Social; Artistic; Investigative. **Skills**—Instructing; learning strategies; writing; speaking; persuasion. **Values**—Social service; social status; autonomy; achievement; recognition. **Work Conditions**—Indoors, environmentally controlled; sitting.

Industrial and Labor Relations

Focuses on employee-management interactions and the management of issues and disputes regarding working conditions and worker benefit packages, and that may prepare individuals to function as labor or personnel relations specialists. **Related CIP Program:** 52.1002 Labor and Industrial Relations.

Specializations in the Major: Arbitration, labor law, mediation, worker compensation, worker safety.

Typical Sequence of College Courses: English composition, business writing, introduction to psychology, principles of microeconomics, principles of macroeconomics, calculus for business and social sciences, statistics for business and social sciences, introduction to management information systems, introduction to accounting, legal environment of business, business finance, introduction to marketing, organizational behavior, human resource management, industrial relations and labor management, employment law, training and development, systems of conflict resolution. **Typical Sequence of High School Courses:** English, algebra, geometry, trigonometry, foreign language, computer science, public speaking, social science.

Career Snapshot: Although labor unions are not as widespread as they once were, they still play an important role in American business. The "just in time" strategy that is popular in the manufacturing and transportation industries means that a strike lasting only a few hours can seriously disrupt business. Employers are eager to settle labor disputes before they start, and this creates job opportunities for labor-relations specialists working for either the employer or the union. Other job openings are found in government agencies that deal with labor. Many of these specialists hold bachelor's degrees, but a master's degree or law degree can be helpful for jobs involving contract negotiations and mediation.

Related Jobs			
Job Title	Average Earnings	Job Growth	Job Openings
1. Business Teachers, Postsecondary	$58,230	32.2%	329,000
2. Compensation and Benefits Managers	$67,040	21.5%	4,000

3. Compensation, Benefits, and Job Analysis Specialists	$48,720	20.4%	15,000
4. Employment Interviewers, Private or Public Employment Service	$41,190	30.5%	30,000
5. Personnel Recruiters	$41,190	30.5%	30,000

Job 1 shares 329,000 job openings with 35 jobs not included in the list. Jobs 4 and 5 share 37,000 job openings.

Characteristics of the Related Jobs: Interests—Enterprising; Social; Conventional. **Skills**—Persuasion; management of personnel resources; negotiation; service orientation; social perceptiveness. **Values**—Social service; working conditions; authority; responsibility; co-workers. **Work Conditions**—Sitting; indoors, environmentally controlled.

Industrial Design

Prepares individuals to use artistic techniques to effectively communicate ideas and information to business and consumer audiences via the creation of effective forms, shapes, and packaging for manufactured products. **Related CIP Program:** 50.0404 Industrial Design.

Specializations in the Major: Computer modeling, product design.

Typical Sequence of College Courses: English composition, college algebra, basic drawing, oral communication, introduction to economics, art history: Renaissance to modern, general physics, introduction to marketing, introduction to graphic design, visual thinking and problem solving, presentation graphics, industrial design materials and processes, human factors in design (ergonomics), computer modeling, history of industrial design, professional practices for industrial design, senior design project. **Typical Sequence of High School Courses:** Algebra, geometry, trigonometry, precalculus, English, public speaking, art, computer science, mechanical drawing, photography.

Career Snapshot: Industrial designers develop every conceivable kind of manufactured product, from cars to computers to children's toys. They need to understand the technology that will make the product work, the human context in which the product will be used—such as the way it will be held in the hand—as well as the marketplace in which the product will compete. Therefore, this field requires students to learn a combination of technical, creative, and business skills. Knowledge of computer-assisted design (CAD) has become essential, and skill with this tool can help in a field that is often keenly competitive and can suffer from outsourcing of work to foreign design firms.

Related Jobs			
Job Title	Average Earnings	Job Growth	Job Openings
1. Art, Drama, and Music Teachers, Postsecondary	$49,740	32.2%	329,000
2. Commercial and Industrial Designers	$52,260	10.8%	7,000
3. Graphic Designers	$37,950	15.2%	35,000

Job 1 shares 329,000 job openings with 35 jobs not included in the list.

Characteristics of the Related Jobs: Interest—Artistic. Skills—Persuasion; instructing; time management; social perceptiveness; coordination. Values—Creativity; ability utilization; achievement; recognition; working conditions. Work Conditions—Sitting; spend time making repetitive motions; indoors, environmentally controlled; noise levels are distracting or uncomfortable.

Industrial Engineering

Focuses on the development and application of complex mathematical or simulation models to solve problems involving operational systems, where the system concerned is subject to human intervention. Related CIP Program: 14.3501 Industrial Engineering.

Specializations in the Major: Operations research, quality control.

Typical Sequence of College Courses: English composition, technical writing, calculus, differential equations, general chemistry, introduction to computer science, general physics, statics, dynamics, numerical analysis, thermodynamics, materials engineering, engineering economics, human factors and ergonomics, engineering systems design, operations research, quality control, facilities design, simulation, analysis of industrial activities,

© JIST Works

senior design project. **Typical Sequence of High School Courses:** English, algebra, geometry, trigonometry, pre-calculus, calculus, chemistry, physics, computer science.

Career Snapshot: Industrial engineers plan how an organization can most efficiently use staff, equipment, buildings, raw materials, information, and energy to output a product or service. They occupy the middle ground between management and the technology experts—for example, the mechanical or chemical engineers. Sometimes they make a career move into management positions. A bachelor's degree is good preparation for this field. The job outlook for industrial engineers is expected to be good, especially in non-manufacturing industries, as U.S. employers attempt to boost productivity to compete in a global workplace.

Related Jobs			
Job Title	Average Earnings	Job Growth	Job Openings
1. Engineering Managers	$99,000	13.0%	15,000
2. Engineering Teachers, Postsecondary	$74,840	32.2%	329,000
3. Industrial Engineers	$66,080	15.9%	13,000

Job 2 shares 329,000 job openings with 35 jobs not included in the list.

Characteristics of the Related Jobs: Interests—Enterprising; Investigative; Realistic. **Skills**—Technology design; management of financial resources; negotiation; science; persuasion. **Values**—Authority: creativity; autonomy; ability utilization; social status; responsibility. **Work Conditions**—Common protective or safety equipment; noise levels are distracting or uncomfortable; hazardous equipment; contaminants; extremely bright or inadequate lighting.

Industrial/Technology Education

Focuses on technological concepts, processes and systems, such as the evolution, utilization and significance of technology as related to industry, and its organization, personnel, systems, techniques, resources and products. **Related CIP Program:** 21.0101 Technology Education/Industrial Arts.

Specializations in the Major: A technology (such as welding), agriculture.

Typical Sequence of College Courses: Introduction to psychology, English composition, oral communication, history and philosophy of education, human growth and development, history and philosophy of industrial education, methods of teaching industrial education, evaluation in industrial education, instructional materials in industrial education, classroom/laboratory management, special needs in industrial education, safety and liability in the classroom, student teaching. **Typical Sequence of High School Courses:** English, algebra, geometry, trigonometry, science, foreign language, industrial arts, mechanical drawing, public speaking.

Career Snapshot: As American industry progresses into a new century, the traditional "shop teacher" is evolving into a technology educator who teaches young people the high-tech skills they need to succeed in the new economy. In industrial/technology education, as in other teaching fields, a bachelor's degree is usually required for job entry, but a master's is often needed to build a career. In addition, it is helpful to get some genuine work experience in industry or agriculture. The job outlook is better for this field than for many other secondary-school specializations. Some graduates pursue careers in sales or training.

Related Jobs			
Job Title	*Average Earnings*	*Job Growth*	*Job Openings*
1. Vocational Education Teachers, Middle School	$43,890	−0.9%	2,000
2. Vocational Education Teachers, Secondary School	$46,650	9.1%	10,000

Characteristics of the Related Jobs: Interest—Social. **Skills**—Instructing; learning strategies; social perceptiveness; service orientation; persuasion. **Values**—Social service; authority; creativity; achievement; responsibility. **Work Conditions**—Standing; noise levels are distracting or uncomfortable; contaminants; walking and running.

© JIST Works

Insurance

Prepares individuals to manage risk in organizational settings and provide insurance and risk-aversion services to businesses, individuals, and other organizations. **Related CIP Program:** 52.1701 Insurance.

Specializations in the Major: Commercial risk management, life and health insurance, property and liability insurance.

Typical Sequence of College Courses: English composition, business writing, introduction to psychology, principles of microeconomics, principles of macroeconomics, calculus for business and social sciences, statistics for business and social sciences, introduction to management information systems, introduction to accounting, legal environment of business, principles of management and organization, operations management, strategic management, business finance, introduction to marketing, property and liability insurance, life and health insurance, commercial risk management, insurance law, employee benefit planning. **Typical Sequence of High School Courses:** English, algebra, geometry, trigonometry, science, foreign language, computer science.

Career Snapshot: A bachelor's degree in insurance may lead to employment in an insurance company or agency as an underwriter or sales agent. Graduates with outstanding mathematical ability may be hired for training as actuaries. Mergers and downsizing among agencies and brokerages may limit the number of job openings.

Related Jobs			
Job Title	*Average Earnings*	*Job Growth*	*Job Openings*
1. Business Teachers, Postsecondary	$58,230	32.2%	329,000
2. Insurance Adjusters, Examiners, and Investigators	$46,060	15.1%	28,000
3. Insurance Appraisers, Auto Damage	$47,790	16.6%	2,000
4. Insurance Sales Agents	$42,030	6.6%	44,000
5. Insurance Underwriters	$49,510	8.0%	13,000

(continued)

(continued)

Job Title	Average Earnings	Job Growth	Job Openings
6. Purchasing Agents, Except Wholesale, Retail, and Farm Products	$48,360	8.1%	19,000
7. Sales Representatives, Wholesale and Manufacturing, Except Technical and Scientific Products	$46,090	12.9%	169,000
8. Telemarketers	$20,460	−10.0%	156,000
9. Wholesale and Retail Buyers, Except Farm Products	$42,190	8.4%	20,000

Job 1 shares 329,000 job openings with 35 jobs not included in the list. Job 2 shares 28,000 job openings with another job not included in the list.

Characteristics of the Related Jobs: Interests—Enterprising; Conventional; Social. **Skills**—Persuasion; negotiation; service orientation; time management; speaking. **Values**—Autonomy; advancement; variety; working conditions; responsibility. **Work Conditions**—Sitting.

Interior Design

Prepares individuals to apply artistic principles and techniques to the professional planning, designing, equipping, and furnishing of residential and commercial interior spaces. **Related CIP Program:** 50.0408 Interior Design.

Specializations in the Major: Acoustics, bathrooms, computer-aided design, kitchens, public spaces, residential design, restoration.

Typical Sequence of College Courses: Basic drawing, history of architecture, introduction to interior design, interior materials, history of interiors, presentation graphics, computer-aided design, color and design, lighting design, interior design studio, construction codes and material rating, senior design project. **Typical Sequence of High School Courses:** English, algebra, literature, history, geometry, art, physics, trigonometry, precalculus, computer science.

© JIST Works

Career Snapshot: Interior designers plan how to shape and decorate the interiors of all kinds of buildings, including homes and commercial structures. They may design new interiors or renovate existing places. They respond to their clients' needs and budgets by developing designs based on traditional forms, innovative uses of layout and materials, sound principles of engineering, and safety codes. A bachelor's degree in the field is not universally required, but it contributes to your qualifications for licensure (in some states) and membership in a professional association and gives you an edge over self-taught competitors.

	Related Jobs		
Job Title	*Average Earnings*	*Job Growth*	*Job Openings*
1. Art, Drama, and Music Teachers, Postsecondary	$49,740	32.2%	329,000
2. Interior Designers	$41,470	15.5%	10,000

Job 1 shares 329,000 job openings with 35 jobs not included in the list.

Characteristics of the Related Jobs: Interests—Artistic; Social; Investigative. **Skills**—Persuasion; instructing; speaking; active learning; social perceptiveness. **Values**—Creativity; social service; ability utilization; authority; achievement. **Work Conditions**—Sitting; indoors, environmentally controlled.

International Business

Prepares individuals to manage international businesses and/or business operations. **Related CIP Program:** 52.1101 International Business/Trade/Commerce.

Specializations in the Major: A particular aspect of business, a particular part of the world.

Typical Sequence of College Courses: English composition, business writing, introduction to psychology, foreign language, principles of microeconomics, principles of macroeconomics, calculus for business and social sciences, statistics for business and social sciences, introduction to management information systems, introduction to accounting, international management, legal environment of business, principles of management and organization, operations management, international economics, business finance, introduction to marketing, organizational behavior, human resource management, international finance. **Typical Sequence of High School Courses:** English, algebra, geometry, trigonometry, science, foreign language, geography, computer science, public speaking.

Career Snapshot: The global economy demands businesspeople who are knowledgeable about other cultures. This major prepares you to work in businesses here and abroad and in the government agencies that deal with them. In addition to studying standard business subjects, you'll probably study or intern abroad to become proficient in a foreign language and gain a global perspective. The work usually requires a lot of travel and a sensitivity to cultural differences.

Related Jobs			
Job Title	*Average Earnings*	*Job Growth*	*Job Openings*
1. Business Teachers, Postsecondary	$58,230	32.2%	329,000
2. Chief Executives	$141,820	14.9%	38,000
3. General and Operations Managers	$79,300	17.0%	208,000
4. Private Sector Executives	$141,820	14.9%	38,000

Job 1 shares 329,000 job openings with 35 jobs not included in the list. Job 4 shares 38,000 job openings with another job not included in the list.

Characteristics of the Related Jobs: Interests—Enterprising; Conventional; Social. **Skills**—Management of financial resources; management of personnel resources; management of material resources; negotiation; coordination. **Values**—Authority; social status; working conditions; creativity; autonomy. **Work Conditions**—Walking and running; indoors, environmentally controlled.

International Relations

Focuses on the systematic study of international politics and institutions, and the conduct of diplomacy and foreign policy. **Related CIP Program:** 45.0901 International Relations and Affairs.

Specializations in the Major: A regional specialization, development, diplomacy, global security, international political economy, U.S. foreign policy.

Typical Sequence of College Courses: English composition, world history to the early modern era, world history in the modern era, introduction to political science, introduction to international relations, foreign language, introduction to economics, microeconomic theory, macroeconomic theory, comparative governments, world regional geography, history of a non-Western civilization, international economics, American foreign policy, seminar (reporting on research). **Typical Sequence of High School Courses:** Algebra, English, foreign language, social science, trigonometry, history.

Career Snapshot: The study of international relations is a multidisciplinary effort that draws on political science, economics, sociology, and history, among other disciplines. It attempts to find meaning in the ways people, private groups, and governments relate to one another politically and economically. The traditional focus on sovereign states is opening up to include attention to other actors on the world stage, including nongovernmental organizations, international organizations, multinational corporations, and groups representing a religion, ethnic group, or ideology. Now that American business is opening to the world more than ever before, this major is gaining in importance. Graduates often go on to law or business school, graduate school in the social sciences, the U.S. Foreign Service, or employment in businesses or organizations with an international focus.

	Related Jobs		
Job Title	*Average Earnings*	*Job Growth*	*Job Openings*
1. Government Service Executives	$141,820	14.9%	38,000
2. Political Science Teachers, Postsecondary	$59,530	32.2%	329,000
3. Political Scientists	$86,460	7.3%	fewer than 500

Job 1 shares 38,000 job openings with another job not included in the list. Job 2 shares 329,000 job openings with 35 jobs not included in the list.

Characteristics of the Related Jobs: Interests—Enterprising; Conventional; Social. **Skills**—Management of financial resources; systems evaluation; systems analysis; management of personnel resources; judgment and decision making. **Values**—Authority; social status; working conditions; creativity;

autonomy. **Work Conditions**—Sitting; indoors, environmentally controlled; walking and running.

Japanese

Focuses on the Japanese language; includes the cultural and historical contexts, dialects, and applications to business, science/technology, and other settings. **Related CIP Program:** 16.0302 Japanese Language and Literature.

Specializations in the Major: History and culture, language education, literature, translation.

Typical Sequence of College Courses: Japanese language, conversation, composition, linguistics, Japanese literature, East Asian literature, East Asian studies, grammar, phonetics. **Typical Sequence of High School Courses:** English, public speaking, foreign language, history, literature, social science.

Career Snapshot: Japan is a major trading partner of the United States, but comparatively few English speakers have mastered the Japanese language. This means that a major in Japanese can be a valuable entry route to careers in international business, travel, and law. A graduate degree in Japanese is good preparation for college teaching or translation.

Related Jobs			
Job Title	Average Earnings	Job Growth	Job Openings
1. Foreign Language and Literature Teachers, Postsecondary	$49,120	32.2%	329,000
2. Interpreters and Translators	$34,900	19.9%	4,000

Job 1 shares 329,000 job openings with 35 jobs not included in the list.

Characteristics of the Related Jobs: Interests—Artistic; Social; Investigative. **Skills**—Writing; active listening; speaking; reading comprehension; service orientation. **Values**—Social service; ability utilization; achievement; autonomy; social status. **Work Conditions**—Sitting; indoors, environmentally controlled.

© JIST Works

Journalism and Mass Communications

Focuses on the theory and practice of gathering, processing, and delivering news and prepares individuals to be professional print journalists, news editors, and news managers. **Related CIP Program:** 09.0401 Journalism.

Specializations in the Major: Media management, news editing and editorializing, news reporting, photojournalism, radio and television news.

Typical Sequence of College Courses: English composition, oral communication, American government, introduction to economics, foreign language, introduction to psychology, introduction to mass communication, writing for mass media, news writing and reporting, copy editing, mass communication law, communication ethics, feature writing, photojournalism, media management, visual design for media. **Typical Sequence of High School Courses:** English, algebra, foreign language, art, literature, public speaking, social science.

Career Snapshot: Journalism is a good preparation not only for news reporting and writing, but also for advertising and (with specialized coursework) news media production. Competition for entry-level journalism jobs can be keen, especially for prestigious newspapers and media outlets. Expect to start in a smaller operation and move around to increasingly bigger employers as you build your career. Although some workers are losing jobs as media outlets merge, new media technologies (such as Web-based magazines) have created some new job openings.

Related Jobs			
Job Title	Average Earnings	Job Growth	Job Openings
1. Broadcast News Analysts	$41,210	4.3%	1,000
2. Caption Writers	$45,460	17.7%	14,000
3. Communications Teachers, Postsecondary	$50,610	32.2%	329,000
4. Copy Writers	$45,460	17.7%	14,000
5. Editors	$44,620	14.8%	16,000
6. Reporters and Correspondents	$31,660	4.9%	4,000

Jobs 2 and 4 share 14,000 job openings. Job 3 shares 329,000 job openings with 35 jobs not included in the list.

Characteristics of the Related Jobs: Interests—Artistic; Enterprising; Social. Skills—Writing; reading comprehension; time management; active listening; critical thinking. Values—Creativity; ability utilization; recognition; achievement; autonomy. Work Conditions—Sitting; indoors, environmentally controlled.

Landscape Architecture

Prepares individuals for the independent professional practice of landscape architecture and research in various aspects of the field. **Related CIP Program:** 04.0601 Landscape Architecture (B.S., B.S.L.A., B.L.A., M.S.L.A., M.L.A., Ph.D.).

Specializations in the Major: Arid lands, eco-tourism, historical and cultural landscapes, international studies, small town and urban revitalization, urban design.

Typical Sequence of College Courses: English composition, calculus, basic drawing, general biology, introduction to soil science, architectural graphics, ecology, history of landscape architecture, landscape architectural design, site analysis, introduction to horticulture, land surveying, landscape structures and materials, architectural computer graphics, land planning, professional practice of landscape architecture, senior design project.
Typical Sequence of High School Courses: English, algebra, geometry, trigonometry, pre-calculus, calculus, physics, computer science, art, biology.

Career Snapshot: Landscape architects must have a good flair for design, ability to work with a variety of construction techniques and technologies, knowledge of the characteristics of many plants, plus business sense. A bachelor's degree is the usual entry route; some people enter the field with a master's degree after a bachelor's in another field. Job opportunities are expected to be good, and an internship is a very helpful credential. About 40 percent of landscape architects are self-employed.

Related Jobs			
Job Title	*Average Earnings*	*Job Growth*	*Job Openings*
1. Architecture Teachers, Postsecondary	$60,400	32.2%	329,000
2. Engineering Managers	$99,000	13.0%	15,000

© JIST Works

3. Landscape Architects	$54,290	19.4%	1,000

Job 1 shares 329,000 job openings with 35 jobs not included in the list.

Characteristics of the Related Jobs: Interests—Enterprising; Realistic; Investigative. **Skills**—Technology design; operations analysis; science; management of financial resources; persuasion. **Values**—Authority; creativity; compensation; autonomy; ability utilization. **Work Conditions**—Common protective or safety equipment; noise levels are distracting or uncomfortable; extremely bright or inadequate lighting; hazardous equipment.

Law

Prepares individuals for the independent professional practice of law, for taking state and national bar examinations, and for advanced research in jurisprudence. **Related CIP Program:** 22.0101 Law (LL.B., J.D.).

Specializations in the Major: Environmental law, family law, intellectual property, international and comparative law, litigation.

Typical Sequence of College Courses: English composition, oral communication, introduction to political science, introduction to philosophy, American history, foreign language, civil procedure, constitutional law, contracts, criminal law, legal communication, legal research, legal writing, property, torts, criminal procedures, evidence, professional responsibility, trusts and estates. **Typical Sequence of High School Courses:** Algebra, English, foreign language, social science, history, geometry, public speaking.

Career Snapshot: Lawyers enter their occupation by completing four years of college, three years of law school, and then passing the bar exam. The undergraduate major may be almost anything that contributes to skills in writing and critical thinking. Often the undergraduate major helps open doors to the kinds of careers that will be options after law school—for example, a bachelor's degree in a business field may help prepare for a career in tax law, labor relations law, or antitrust law. Graduates of law school can expect keen competition for positions as lawyers. Most openings are expected to be for staff lawyers rather than self-employed lawyers. In addition, many law school graduates take business and government jobs where they use knowledge of law but do not practice it.

© JIST Works

Related Jobs			
Job Title	Average Earnings	Job Growth	Job Openings
1. Administrative Law Judges, Adjudicators, and Hearing Officers	$68,720	10.1%	1,000
2. Arbitrators, Mediators, and Conciliators	$53,690	15.5%	fewer than 500
3. Judges, Magistrate Judges, and Magistrates	$97,260	6.9%	1,000
4. Law Clerks	$34,560	7.7%	7,000
5. Law Teachers, Postsecondary	$89,000	32.2%	329,000
6. Lawyers	$97,420	15.0%	40,000

Job 5 shares 329,000 job openings with 35 jobs not included in the list.

Characteristics of the Related Jobs: Interest—Enterprising. **Skills**—Persuasion; negotiation; critical thinking; writing; judgment and decision making. **Values**—Autonomy; social service; ability utilization; compensation; creativity. **Work Conditions**—Sitting; indoors, environmentally controlled.

Library Science

Focuses on the knowledge and skills required to develop, organize, store, retrieve, administer, and facilitate the use of local, remote, and networked collections of information in print, audiovisual, and electronic formats and that prepares individuals for professional service as librarians and information consultants. **Related CIP Program:** 25.0101 Library Science/ Librarianship.

Specializations in the Major: Archives, cataloguing, children's libraries, instructional libraries, map libraries, music libraries, online information retrieval, special interest libraries.

Typical Sequence of College Courses: English composition, oral communication, introduction to computer science, foreign language, introduction to library and information science, reference services and resources, management of libraries and information services, bibliographic control of library materials, library research and evaluation. **Typical Sequence of High**

© JIST Works

School Courses: English, foreign language, computer science, algebra, public speaking, office computer applications, keyboarding, social science.

Career Snapshot: This major is sometimes called library and information science because increasingly the information that is needed by businesses, governments, and individuals is not available in books. Library science programs teach not only how to serve library users and manage library collections, but also how to retrieve and compile information from online databases. The master's degree is the entry-level credential in this field; a special librarian often needs an additional graduate or professional degree. Master's degree programs prefer applicants who have a bachelor's in a different field. The best employment opportunities will probably be in online information retrieval and in nontraditional settings.

Related Jobs			
Job Title	Average Earnings	Job Growth	Job Openings
1. Librarians	$46,940	4.9%	8,000
2. Library Science Teachers, Postsecondary	$52,490	32.2%	329,000

Job 2 shares 329,000 job openings with 35 jobs not included in the list.

Characteristics of the Related Jobs: Interests—Artistic; Conventional; Investigative. **Skills**—Management of financial resources; learning strategies; persuasion; service orientation; management of material resources. **Values**—Authority; working conditions; social service; co-workers; responsibility. **Work Conditions**—Indoors, environmentally controlled; sitting; spend time making repetitive motions.

Management Information Systems

Prepares individuals to provide and manage data systems and related facilities for processing and retrieving internal business information; select systems and train personnel; and respond to external data requests. **Related CIP Program:** 52.1201 Management Information Systems, General.

Specializations in the Major: Accounting, network programming, security and disaster recovery.

Typical Sequence of College Courses: English composition, business writing, introduction to psychology, principles of microeconomics, principles of macroeconomics, calculus for business and social sciences, statistics for business and social sciences, introduction to management information systems, introduction to accounting, legal environment of business, principles of management and organization, operations management, strategic management, business finance, introduction to marketing, database management systems, systems analysis and design, decision support systems for management, networks and telecommunications. **Typical Sequence of High School Courses:** English, algebra, geometry, trigonometry, science, foreign language, computer science.

Career Snapshot: The management information systems major is considered a business major, which means that students get a firm grounding in economics, accounting, business law, finance, and marketing, as well as the technical skills needed to work with the latest business computer applications. Students may specialize in MIS at either the bachelor's or master's level and may combine it with a degree in a related business field, such as accounting or finance, or in computer science. The job outlook is very good.

Related Jobs			
Job Title	Average Earnings	Job Growth	Job Openings
1. Computer and Information Systems Managers	$94,390	25.9%	25,000
2. Computer Programmers	$62,980	2.0%	28,000
3. Database Administrators	$61,950	38.2%	9,000

Characteristics of the Related Jobs: Interests—Investigative; Conventional; Realistic. **Skills**—Programming; operations analysis; technology design; systems analysis; troubleshooting. **Values**—Creativity; authority; ability utilization; compensation; advancement. **Work Conditions**—Sitting; spend time making repetitive motions; indoors, environmentally controlled.

© JIST Works

Marketing

Prepares individuals to undertake and manage the process of developing consumer audiences and moving products from producers to consumers. **Related CIP Program:** 52.1401 Marketing/Marketing Management, General.

Specializations in the Major: Marketing management, marketing research.

Typical Sequence of College Courses: English composition, business writing, introduction to psychology, principles of microeconomics, principles of macroeconomics, calculus for business and social sciences, statistics for business and social sciences, introduction to management information systems, introduction to accounting, legal environment of business, principles of management and organization, operations management, strategic management, business finance, introduction to marketing, marketing research, buyer behavior, decision support systems for management, marketing strategy.

Typical Sequence of High School Courses: English, algebra, geometry, trigonometry, science, foreign language, computer science.

Career Snapshot: Marketing is the study of how buyers and sellers of goods and services find one another, how businesses can tailor their offerings to meet demand, and how businesses can anticipate and influence demand. It uses the findings of economics, psychology, and sociology in a business context. A bachelor's degree is good preparation for a job in marketing research. Usually some experience in this field is required before a person can move into a marketing management position. Job outlook varies, with some industries looking more favorable than others.

Related Jobs			
Job Title	Average Earnings	Job Growth	Job Openings
1. Advertising and Promotions Managers	$66,560	20.3%	9,000
2. Business Teachers, Postsecondary	$58,230	32.2%	329,000
3. Marketing Managers	$90,450	20.8%	23,000
4. Sales Managers	$85,980	19.7%	40,000

Job 2 shares 329,000 job openings with 35 jobs not included in the list.

Characteristics of the Related Jobs: Interests—Enterprising; Conventional. Skills—Management of personnel resources; negotiation; persuasion; service orientation; management of financial resources. Values—Authority; creativity; working conditions; compensation; autonomy. Work Conditions—Sitting; indoors, environmentally controlled.

Materials Science

Focuses on the general application of mathematical and scientific principles to the analysis and evaluation of the characteristics and behavior of solids. Related CIP Program: 14.3101 Materials Science.

Specializations in the Major: Building materials, ceramics/glass, polymers, thin films.

Typical Sequence of College Courses: English composition, technical writing, calculus, differential equations, introduction to computer science, general chemistry, physical chemistry, general physics, thermodynamics, numerical analysis, introduction to electric circuits, statics, dynamics, phase equilibrium, introduction to materials science, mechanics of materials, microstructure and mechanical properties, materials characterization, kinetics of chemical and physical reactions, senior design project. Typical Sequence of High School Courses: English, algebra, geometry, trigonometry, pre-calculus, calculus, chemistry, physics, computer science.

Career Snapshot: Materials scientists research the physical and chemical properties of ceramics, plastics, and other materials. They devise technologically elegant and economically valuable ways of creating and forming these materials. A bachelor's degree is a common entry route to this field, although those who want to do basic research or teach in college will need to get an advanced degree. The job outlook is best for those working exotic materials, such as nanomaterials (extremely small) or biomaterials.

Related Jobs			
Job Title	Average Earnings	Job Growth	Job Openings
1. Engineering Managers	$99,000	13.0%	15,000
2. Engineering Teachers, Postsecondary	$74,840	32.2%	329,000

© JIST Works

| 3. Materials Scientists | $70,410 | 8.0% | fewer than 500 |

Job 2 shares 329,000 job openings with 35 jobs not included in the list.

Characteristics of the Related Jobs: Interests—Enterprising; Investigative; Realistic. **Skills**—Science; technology design; operations analysis; management of financial resources; mathematics. **Values**—Authority; creativity; autonomy; compensation; ability utilization. **Work Conditions**—Common protective or safety equipment; noise levels are distracting or uncomfortable; sitting; extremely bright or inadequate lighting; hazardous equipment.

Mathematics

Focuses on the analysis of quantities, magnitudes, forms, and their relationships, using symbolic logic and language. **Related CIP Program:** 27.0101 Mathematics, General.

Specializations in the Major: Applied mathematics, mathematical statistics, mathematics education, theoretical mathematics.

Typical Sequence of College Courses: Calculus, differential equations, introduction to computer science, programming in a language (e.g., C, PASCAL, COBOL), statistics, linear algebra, introduction to abstract mathematics. **Typical Sequence of High School Courses:** Algebra, geometry, trigonometry, pre-calculus, calculus, computer science, physics.

Career Snapshot: Mathematics is a science in its own right, in which researchers with graduate degrees continue to discover new laws. It is also a tool for understanding and organizing many aspects of our world. Many mathematics majors apply their knowledge by getting additional education or training in a math-intense field, either in a master's program or on the job. For example, an insurance company might train them in actuarial science; a computer consulting company might train them in computer security; a bank might train them in financial modeling; they might get an economics, engineering, or accounting degree. Employment opportunities are very good for people who apply mathematical knowledge to other fields.

Related Jobs			
Job Title	Average Earnings	Job Growth	Job Openings
1. Mathematical Science Teachers, Postsecondary	$53,250	32.2%	329,000
2. Mathematicians	$81,010	–1.3%	fewer than 500
3. Natural Sciences Managers	$90,080	13.6%	5,000
4. Statisticians	$59,960	4.6%	2,000

Job 1 shares 329,000 job openings with 35 jobs not included in the list.

Characteristics of the Related Jobs: Interests—Investigative; Conventional; Realistic. Skills—Mathematics; science; active learning; critical thinking; complex problem solving. Values—Authority; creativity; autonomy; ability utilization; working conditions. Work Conditions—Indoors, environmentally controlled; sitting.

Mechanical Engineering

Prepares individuals to apply mathematical and scientific principles to the design, development and operational evaluation of physical systems used in manufacturing and end-product systems used for specific uses. Related CIP Program: 14.1901 Mechanical Engineering.

Specializations in the Major: Automotive design, heating and air conditioning, testing.

Typical Sequence of College Courses: English composition, technical writing, calculus, differential equations, general chemistry, introduction to computer science, general physics, introduction to engineering, statics, dynamics, thermodynamics, numerical analysis, fluid mechanics, materials science, materials engineering, mechanical engineering design, heat transfer, manufacturing processes, senior design project. Typical Sequence of High School Courses: English, algebra, geometry, trigonometry, pre-calculus, calculus, chemistry, physics, computer science.

Career Snapshot: Mechanical engineers design, test, and supervise the manufacture of various mechanical devices, including tools, motors, machines, and medical equipment. Their goal is to maximize both the technical efficiency and the economic benefits of the devices. Usually they

© JIST Works

enter their first job with a bachelor's degree. Sometimes they move from engineering to a managerial position. Despite an expected decline in manufacturing, job opportunities are expected to be good because of increasing emphasis on efficiency.

Related Jobs			
Job Title	Average Earnings	Job Growth	Job Openings
1. Cost Estimators	$50,920	18.2%	15,000
2. Engineering Managers	$99,000	13.0%	15,000
3. Engineering Teachers, Postsecondary	$74,840	32.2%	329,000
4. Mechanical Engineers	$67,220	11.1%	11,000

Job 3 shares 329,000 job openings with 35 jobs not included in the list.

Characteristics of the Related Jobs: Interests—Realistic; Enterprising; Conventional. **Skills**—Operations analysis; science; management of financial resources; mathematics; negotiation. **Values**—Autonomy; working conditions; authority; responsibility; creativity. **Work Conditions**—Hazardous equipment; common protective or safety equipment; sitting; indoors, environmentally controlled.

Medical Technology

Prepares individuals to conduct and supervise complex medical tests, clinical trials, and research experiments; manage clinical laboratories; and consult with physicians and clinical researchers on diagnoses, disease causation and spread, and research outcomes. **Related CIP Program:** 51.1005 Clinical Laboratory Science/Medical Technology/Technologist.

Specializations in the Major: Blood banking, body fluid analysis, clinical chemistry, clinical microbiology, hematology, immunology.

Typical Sequence of College Courses: English composition, general biology, general chemistry, organic chemistry, human anatomy and physiology, general microbiology, introduction to biochemistry, college algebra, introduction to computer science, statistics, body fluid analysis, parasitology, clinical chemistry, hematology and coagulation, clinical microbiology, immunohematology, clinical immunology and serology, medical technology education, medical technology management and supervision. **Typical**

Sequence of High School Courses: Algebra, biology, chemistry, computer science, English, physics, geometry, trigonometry.

Career Snapshot: The detection, diagnosis, and prevention of disease depend heavily on various kinds of medical tests—of blood, urine, tissue samples, and so on. Medical technologists, also called clinical laboratory scientists, are trained to perform these tests after studying the principles of chemistry, microbiology, and other basic sciences, plus laboratory techniques that sometimes involve complex and sophisticated equipment. A bachelor's degree is the usual preparation. Job outlook is generally good.

Related Jobs			
Job Title	Average Earnings	Job Growth	Job Openings
1. Health Specialties Teachers, Postsecondary	$70,310	32.2%	329,000
2. Medical and Clinical Laboratory Technologists	$46,710	20.5%	14,000

Job 1 shares 329,000 job openings with 35 jobs not included in the list.

Characteristics of the Related Jobs: Interests—Investigative; Realistic; Social. **Skills**—Science; instructing; critical thinking; active learning; quality control analysis. **Values**—Social service; authority; ability utilization; achievement; social status. **Work Conditions**—Exposed to disease or infections; hazardous conditions; common protective or safety equipment; contaminants; indoors, environmentally controlled.

Medicine

Prepares individuals for the independent professional practice of medicine, involving the prevention, diagnosis, and treatment of illnesses, injuries, and other disorders of the human body. **Related CIP Programs:** 51.1201 Medicine (M.D.); 51.1901 Osteopathic Medicine/Osteopathy (D.O.).

Specializations in the Major: Emergency medicine, family medicine, internal medicine, obstetrics/gynecology, pediatrics, psychiatry, radiology, surgery.

Typical Sequence of College Courses: English composition, introduction to psychology, college algebra, calculus, introduction to sociology, oral

© JIST Works

communication, general chemistry, general biology, introduction to computer science, organic chemistry, human anatomy and physiology, general microbiology, genetics, introduction to biochemistry, pathology, pharmacology, abnormal psychology, medical interviewing techniques, patient examination and evaluation, clinical laboratory procedures, ethics in health care, clinical experience in internal medicine, clinical experience in emergency medicine, clinical experience in obstetrics/gynecology, clinical experience in family medicine, clinical experience in psychiatry, clinical experience in surgery, clinical experience in pediatrics, clinical experience in geriatrics. **Typical Sequence of High School Courses:** English, algebra, geometry, trigonometry, pre-calculus, biology, computer science, public speaking, chemistry, foreign language, physics.

Career Snapshot: Medicine requires long years of education—four years of college, four years of medical school, and three to eight years of internship and residency, depending on the specialty. Entrance to medical school is highly competitive. Although "pre-med" is often referred to as a major, many students meet the entry requirements for medical school while majoring in a nonscientific subject. This may be helpful to demonstrate that you are a well-rounded person and to prepare you for another career in case you are not admitted to medical school. Today, physicians are more likely than in the past to work as salaried employees of group practices or HMOs. Best opportunities are expected in rural and low-income areas.

Related Jobs			
Job Title	*Average Earnings*	*Job Growth*	*Job Openings*
1. Anesthesiologists	more than $145,600	24.0%	41,000
2. Family and General Practitioners	$136,170	24.0%	41,000
3. Internists, General	more than $145,600	24.0%	41,000
4. Obstetricians and Gynecologists	more than $145,600	24.0%	41,000
5. Pediatricians, General	$135,450	24.0%	41,000
6. Psychiatrists	more than $145,600	24.0%	41,000
7. Surgeons	more than $145,600	24.0%	41,000

These 7 jobs share 41,000 job openings.

Characteristics of the Related Jobs: Interests—Investigative; Social; Realistic. Skills—Science; social perceptiveness; persuasion; instructing; service orientation. Values—Social service; social status; recognition; ability utilization; responsibility. Work Conditions—Exposed to disease or infections; common protective or safety equipment; exposed to radiation; specialized protective or safety equipment; indoors, environmentally controlled.

Metallurgical Engineering

Prepares individuals to apply mathematical and metallurgical principles to the design, development and operational evaluation of metal components of structural, load-bearing, power, transmission, and moving systems. Related CIP Program: 14.2001 Metallurgical Engineering.

Specializations in the Major: Chemical metallurgy, materials research, physical metallurgy, process engineering.

Typical Sequence of College Courses: English composition, calculus, differential equations, general chemistry, introduction to computer science, general physics, organic chemistry, introduction to electric circuits, thermodynamics, numerical analysis, materials engineering, materials thermodynamics, physics of metals, hydroprocessing of materials, metallurgical transport phenomena, metallurgical design, mechanical metallurgy, process modeling, optimization and control, senior design project. Typical Sequence of High School Courses: English, algebra, geometry, trigonometry, pre-calculus, calculus, chemistry, physics, computer science.

Career Snapshot: Metallurgy is the science of refining and alloying metals, and shaping them to form structures and products. Metallurgical engineers apply principles of physics, chemistry, materials science, and economics to improve extractive and manufacturing processes. A bachelor's degree is often an entry route to this field, which may eventually lead to management. Best job growth in this field is expected for those who work with nanotechnology (extremely small materials).

© JIST Works

Related Jobs			
Job Title	Average Earnings	Job Growth	Job Openings
1. Engineering Managers	$99,000	13.0%	15,000
2. Engineering Teachers, Postsecondary	$74,840	32.2%	329,000
3. Materials Engineers	$68,570	12.2%	2,000

Job 2 shares 329,000 job openings with 35 jobs not included in the list.

Characteristics of the Related Jobs: Interests—Enterprising; Investigative; Realistic. **Skills**—Technology design; science; operations analysis; management of financial resources; mathematics. **Values**—Authority; creativity; autonomy; compensation; ability utilization. **Work Conditions**—Common protective or safety equipment; sitting; noise levels are distracting or uncomfortable; extremely bright or inadequate lighting; hazardous equipment.

Microbiology

Focuses on the scientific study of one-celled organisms and colonies, and subcellular genetic matter and their ecological interactions with human beings and other life. **Related CIP Programs:** 26.0503 Medical Microbiology and Bacteriology; 26.0502 Microbiology, General; 26.0506 Mycology; 26.0505 Parasitology; 26.0504 Virology.

Specializations in the Major: Algae, bacteria, fungi (mycology), immunology, virology.

Typical Sequence of College Courses: English composition, calculus, introduction to computer science, general chemistry, general biology, organic chemistry, general physics, general microbiology, genetics, introduction to biochemistry, immunology, bacterial physiology, bacterial genetics. **Typical Sequence of High School Courses:** English, biology, algebra, geometry, trigonometry, pre-calculus, chemistry, physics, computer science, calculus.

Career Snapshot: A bachelor's degree in microbiology or bacteriology may be an entry route to clinical laboratory work or to nonresearch work in industry or government. It also is good preparation for medical school. For a position in research or college teaching, a graduate degree is expected.

Related Jobs			
Job Title	Average Earnings	Job Growth	Job Openings
1. Biological Science Teachers, Postsecondary	$63,750	32.2%	329,000
2. Medical Scientists, Except Epidemiologists	$60,240	34.1%	15,000
3. Microbiologists	$55,300	17.2%	1,000
4. Natural Sciences Managers	$90,080	13.6%	5,000

Job 1 shares 329,000 job openings with 35 jobs not included in the list.

Characteristics of the Related Jobs: Interest—Investigative. **Skills**—Science; instructing; reading comprehension; writing; active learning. **Values**—Creativity; social status; authority; ability utilization; autonomy. **Work Conditions**—Exposed to disease or infections; indoors, environmentally controlled; hazardous conditions; sitting; specialized protective or safety equipment.

Modern Foreign Language

Focuses on a language being used in the modern world and includes related dialects, the cultural and historical contexts, and applications to business, science/technology, and other settings. **Related CIP Programs:** 16.0201 African Languages, Literatures, and Linguistics; 16.0404 Albanian Language and Literature; 16.1001 American Indian/Native American Languages, Literatures, and Linguistics; 16.1101 Arabic Language and Literature; 16.1401 Australian/Oceanic/Pacific Languages, Literatures, and Linguistics; 16.1402 Bahasa Indonesian/Bahasa Malay Languages and Literatures; 16.0401 Baltic Languages, Literatures, and Linguistics; 16.0704 Bengali Language and Literature; 16.0405 Bulgarian Language and Literature; 16.1403 Burmese Language and Literature; 16.0907 Catalan Language and Literature; 16.1301 Celtic Languages, Literatures, and Linguistics; 16.0301 Chinese Language and Literature; 16.0406 Czech Language and Literature; 16.0503 Danish Language and Literature; 16.0504 Dutch/Flemish Language and Literature; 16.0300 East Asian Languages, Literatures, and Linguistics, General; 16.1404 Filipino/Tagalog

© JIST Works

Language and Literature; 16.1502 Finnish and Related Languages, Literatures, and Linguistics; 16.0901 French Language and Literature; 16.0501 German Language and Literature; others.

Specializations in the Major: History and culture, language education, literature, regional studies, translation.

Typical Sequence of College Courses: Foreign language, conversation, composition, linguistics, foreign literature and culture, grammar, phonetics, history of a world region. **Typical Sequence of High School Courses:** English, public speaking, foreign language, history, social science.

Career Snapshot: The most popular foreign language majors—Chinese, French, German, Japanese, Russian, and Spanish—are described elsewhere in this book. But many colleges offer majors in other modern languages, such as Arabic, Hebrew, Hindi, Portuguese, Swahili, Swedish, or Turkish, to name just a few. As global trade continues to increase, a degree in a foreign language can lead to many job opportunities in international business, travel, and law. Many employers are looking for graduates with an understanding of a second language and culture. Translation or college teaching are options for those with a graduate degree in a foreign language.

Related Jobs			
Job Title	*Average Earnings*	*Job Growth*	*Job Openings*
1. Foreign Language and Literature Teachers, Postsecondary	$49,120	32.2%	329,000
2. Interpreters and Translators	$34,900	19.9%	4,000
Job 1 shares 329,000 job openings with 35 jobs not included in the list.			

Characteristics of the Related Jobs: Interests—Artistic; Social; Investigative. **Skills**—Writing; active listening; speaking; reading comprehension; service orientation. **Values**—Social service; ability utilization; achievement; autonomy; social status. **Work Conditions**—Sitting; indoors, environmentally controlled.

Music

Prepares individuals to master musical instruments and performing art as solo and/or ensemble performers, or to be creators or arrangers of music. **Related CIP Programs:** 50.0906 Conducting; 50.0910 Jazz/Jazz Studies; 50.0902 Music History, Literature, and Theory; 50.0909 Music Management and Merchandising; 50.0912 Music Pedagogy; 50.0903 Music Performance, General; 50.0904 Music Theory and Composition; 50.0901 Music, General; 50.0905 Musicology and Ethnomusicology; 50.0907 Piano and Organ; 50.0911 Violin, Viola, Guitar, and Other Stringed Instruments; 50.0908 Voice and Opera.

Specializations in the Major: Composition, music education, music theory, performance.

Typical Sequence of College Courses: English composition, foreign language, piano proficiency, introduction to music theory, harmony and counterpoint, conducting, music history and literature, recital attendance, performance technique with instrument/voice, recital performance. **Typical Sequence of High School Courses:** Music, foreign language, English.

Career Snapshot: Music majors study theory, composition, and performance. They learn how the success of a work of music depends on certain principles of what appeals to the ear, on the skill of the arranger, and on the interpretation of the performers. Relatively few graduates are able to support themselves as composers, arrangers, or performers, but many teach in schools or universities or give private instruction.

Related Jobs			
Job Title	Average Earnings	Job Growth	Job Openings
1. Art, Drama, and Music Teachers, Postsecondary	$49,740	32.2%	329,000
2. Composers	$34,800	10.4%	11,000
3. Music Arrangers and Orchestrators	$34,800	10.4%	11,000
4. Music Directors	$34,800	10.4%	11,000
5. Musicians, Instrumental	No data available	14.0%	37,000
6. Singers	No data available	14.0%	37,000

Job 1 shares 329,000 job openings with 35 jobs not included in the list. Jobs 2, 3, and 4 share 11,000 job openings. Jobs 5 and 6 share 37,000 job openings.

© JIST Works

Characteristics of the Related Jobs: Interests—Artistic; Social; Investigative. Skills—Coordination; speaking; instructing; monitoring; active learning. Values—Ability utilization; creativity; achievement; recognition; autonomy. Work Conditions—Sitting; indoors, environmentally controlled.

Nursing (R.N. Training)

Prepares individuals in the knowledge, techniques and procedures for promoting health, providing care for sick, disabled, informed, or other individuals or groups. Related CIP Program: 51.1601 Nursing/Registered Nurse (R.N., A.S.N., B.S.N., M.S.N.).

Specializations in the Major: Community health nursing, mental health nursing, nursing administration, pediatric nursing.

Typical Sequence of College Courses: English composition, introduction to psychology, college algebra, introduction to sociology, oral communication, general chemistry, general biology, human anatomy and physiology, general microbiology, ethics in health care, patient examination and evaluation, pharmacology, reproductive health nursing, pediatric nursing, adult health nursing, mental health nursing, nursing leadership and management, community health nursing, clinical nursing experience. Typical Sequence of High School Courses: English, algebra, geometry, trigonometry, biology, computer science, public speaking, chemistry, foreign language.

Career Snapshot: The study of nursing includes a combination of classroom and clinical work. Students learn what science tells us about the origins and treatment of disease, how to care effectively for the physical and emotional needs of sick and injured people, and how to teach people to maintain health. Nurses work in a variety of health care settings, including physicians' offices, patients' homes, schools and companies, and in desk jobs for HMOs. The employment outlook is excellent in all specialties.

Related Jobs			
Job Title	Average Earnings	Job Growth	Job Openings
1. Nursing Instructors and Teachers, Postsecondary	$52,720	32.2%	329,000
2. Registered Nurses	$53,640	29.4%	229,000
Job 1 shares 329,000 job openings with 35 jobs not included in the list.			

Characteristics of the Related Jobs: Interests—Social; Investigative; Realistic. Skills—Social perceptiveness; service orientation; time management; instructing; science. Values—Social service; co-workers; ability utilization; achievement; activity. Work Conditions—Exposed to disease or infections; common protective or safety equipment; exposed to radiation; cramped work space, awkward positions; contaminants.

Occupational Health and Industrial Hygiene

Prepares public health specialists to monitor and evaluate health and related safety standards in industrial, commercial, and government workplaces and facilities. Related CIP Program: 51.2206 Occupational Health and Industrial Hygiene.

Specializations in the Major: Hazardous materials, occupational health, safety.

Typical Sequence of College Courses: English composition, oral communication, calculus, technical writing, general chemistry, introduction to computer science, general physics, general biology, introduction to environmental health, introduction to occupational health and safety, biostatistics, organic chemistry, pollution science and treatment, statistics, microbial hazards, chemistry of hazardous materials, safety organization and management, industrial fire prevention, occupational safety and health law, environmental regulations. Typical Sequence of High School Courses: English, algebra, geometry, trigonometry, pre-calculus, chemistry, physics, computer science, public speaking.

Career Snapshot: Graduates with a bachelor's or master's degree in occupational health and industrial hygiene are trained to protect workers from a variety of threats to their health and safety: chemical and biological contaminants, fire, noise, cramped bodily positions, dangerous machinery, and radiation. The major covers the nature of the risks from these and other hazards, the laws that exist to ban such hazards, how to recognize the presence and assess the risks of workplace hazards, and how to take steps to eliminate them. It is possible to get a job as a technician with an associate's degree, but the federal government and many other employers require a bachelor's. Most job opportunities are in the private sector and are somewhat sensitive to economic ups and downs, but government jobs are much more secure.

© JIST Works

Related Jobs			
Job Title	Average Earnings	Job Growth	Job Openings
1. Health Specialties Teachers, Postsecondary	$70,310	32.2%	329,000
2. Occupational Health and Safety Specialists	$52,640	12.4%	3,000

Job 1 shares 329,000 job openings with 35 jobs not included in the list.

Characteristics of the Related Jobs: **Interests**—Investigative; Social. **Skills**—Science; instructing; writing; speaking; reading comprehension. **Values**—Authority; social service; creativity; autonomy; social status. **Work Conditions**—Exposed to disease or infections; indoors, environmentally controlled; sitting; exposed to radiation; hazardous conditions.

Occupational Therapy

Prepares individuals to assist patients limited by physical, cognitive, psychosocial, mental, developmental, and learning disabilities, as well as adverse environmental conditions, to maximize their independence and maintain optimum health through a planned mix of acquired skills, performance motivation, environmental adaptations, assistive technologies, and physical agents. **Related CIP Program:** 51.2306 Occupational Therapy/Therapist.

Specializations in the Major: Geriatric OT, pediatric OT, prosthetics.

Typical Sequence of College Courses: English composition, statistics for business and social sciences, general chemistry, general biology, human anatomy and physiology, introduction to psychology, human growth and development, introduction to computer science, abnormal psychology, fundamentals of medical science, neuroscience for therapy, occupational therapy for developmental problems, occupational therapy for physiological diagnoses, occupational therapy for psychosocial diagnoses, administration of occupational therapy services, research methods in occupational therapy, methods of facilitating therapeutic adaptation, occupational therapy fieldwork experience, seminar (reporting on research). **Typical Sequence of High School Courses:** English, algebra, geometry, trigonometry, chemistry, physics, biology, foreign language, computer science.

Career Snapshot: Occupational therapists help people cope with disabilities and lead more productive and enjoyable lives. Some therapists enter the field with a bachelor's degree in occupational therapy; others get a master's after a bachelor's in another field. They learn about the nature of various kinds of disabilities—developmental, emotional, and so on—and how to help people overcome them or compensate for them in their daily lives. The long-range outlook for jobs is considered quite good, although in the short run it may be affected by cutbacks in Medicare coverage of therapies.

Related Jobs			
Job Title	Average Earnings	Job Growth	Job Openings
1. Health Specialties Teachers, Postsecondary	$70,310	32.2%	329,000
2. Occupational Therapists	$55,640	33.6%	7,000

Job 1 shares 329,000 job openings with 35 jobs not included in the list.

Characteristics of the Related Jobs: Interests—Social; Investigative; Realistic. **Skills**—Science; instructing; learning strategies; social perceptiveness; writing. **Values**—Social service; authority; achievement; creativity; ability utilization. **Work Conditions**—Exposed to disease or infections; indoors, environmentally controlled; sitting.

Oceanography

Focuses on the scientific study of the ecology and behavior of microbes, plants, and animals inhabiting oceans, coastal waters, and saltwater wetlands; and the chemical components, mechanisms, structure, and movement of ocean waters and their interaction with terrestrial and atmospheric phenomena. **Related CIP Programs:** 26.1302 Marine Biology and Biological Oceanography; 40.0607 Oceanography, Chemical and Physical.

Specializations in the Major: Ocean biology, ocean chemistry, ocean geology, ocean meteorology.

Typical Sequence of College Courses: English composition, introduction to computer science, calculus, differential equations, general chemistry, general physics, agricultural power and machines, physical oceanography, chemical oceanography, geological oceanography, biological oceanography,

© JIST Works

seminar (reporting on research). **Typical Sequence of High School Courses:** English, algebra, geometry, trigonometry, chemistry, pre-calculus, physics, computer science, biology, calculus.

Career Snapshot: Oceans cover more of the earth than does dry land, yet many of the physical and biological characteristics of the oceans are poorly understood. Oceanographers use techniques of physical sciences to study the properties of ocean waters and how these affect coastal areas, climate, and weather. Those who specialize in ocean life work to improve the fishing industry, to protect the environment, and to understand the relationship between oceanic and terrestrial life forms. It is possible to get started in this field with a bachelor's degree; for advancement and many research jobs, however, a master's degree or Ph.D. is helpful or required.

Related Jobs			
Job Title	Average Earnings	Job Growth	Job Openings
1. Atmospheric, Earth, Marine, and Space Sciences Teachers, Postsecondary	$65,250	32.2%	329,000
2. Biological Science Teachers, Postsecondary	$63,750	32.2%	329,000
3. Geologists	$70,180	8.3%	2,000
4. Geoscientists, Except Hydrologists and Geographers	$70,180	8.3%	2,000
5. Hydrologists	$60,880	31.6%	1,000
6. Natural Sciences Managers	$90,080	13.6%	5,000

Jobs 1 and 2 share 329,000 job openings with each other and with 34 jobs not included in the list.

Characteristics of the Related Jobs: Interest—Investigative. **Skills**— Science; active learning; critical thinking; writing; instructing. **Values**— Creativity; authority; responsibility; autonomy; ability utilization. **Work Conditions**—Hazardous conditions; indoors, environmentally controlled; sitting; contaminants; specialized protective or safety equipment.

Operations Management

Prepares individuals to manage and direct the physical and/or technical functions of a firm or organization, particularly those relating to development, production, and manufacturing. **Related CIP Programs:** 52.0203 Logistics and Materials Management; 52.0205 Operations Management and Supervision.

Specializations in the Major: Logistics, materials management, process analysis, production supervision, quality assurance.

Typical Sequence of College Courses: English composition, business writing, introduction to psychology, principles of microeconomics, principles of macroeconomics, calculus for business and social sciences, statistics for business and social sciences, introduction to management information systems, introduction to accounting, legal environment of business, principles of management and organization, operations management, business finance, introduction to marketing, introduction to logistics, organizational behavior, human resource management, ancient literate civilizations, inventory management, supply chain management. **Typical Sequence of High School Courses:** English, algebra, geometry, trigonometry, science, pre-calculus, computer science.

Career Snapshot: Whereas other managers focus on segments of the production and distribution process (such as marketing or finance), operations managers look at the entire process and devise ways to streamline it. They use quantitative methods and computer technology to study the inputs of materials, energy, and labor into production, the processes that create products, and the paths that products take to reach customers. Their skills are greatly valued in today's competitive global business environment.

Related Jobs			
Job Title	Average Earnings	Job Growth	Job Openings
1. Business Teachers, Postsecondary	$58,230	32.2%	329,000
2. Computer and Information Systems Managers	$94,390	25.9%	25,000
3. Construction Managers	$70,770	10.4%	28,000

© JIST Works

4. First-Line Supervisors/ Managers of Mechanics, Installers, and Repairers	$51,000	12.4%	33,000
5. First-Line Supervisors/ Managers of Production and Operating Workers	$45,230	2.7%	89,000
6. Industrial Production Managers	$74,100	0.8%	13,000
7. Logisticians	$59,460	13.2%	7,000
8. Storage and Distribution Managers	$67,300	12.7%	15,000
9. Transportation Managers	$67,300	12.7%	15,000

Job 1 shares 329,000 job openings with 35 jobs not included in the list. Jobs 8 and 9 share 15,000 job openings.

Characteristics of the Related Jobs: Interests—Enterprising; Conventional; Realistic. **Skills**—Management of personnel resources; management of material resources; persuasion; negotiation; management of financial resources. **Values**—Authority; responsibility; autonomy; variety; creativity. **Work Conditions**—Common protective or safety equipment; noise levels are distracting or uncomfortable; contaminants; hazardous equipment.

Optometry

Focuses on the principles and techniques for examining, diagnosing and treating conditions of the visual system. **Related CIP Program:** 51.1701 Optometry (O.D.).

Specializations in the Major: Contact lenses, low vision.

Typical Sequence of College Courses: English composition, introduction to psychology, calculus, introduction to sociology, oral communication, general chemistry, general biology, organic chemistry, general microbiology, introduction to biochemistry, microbiology for optometry, geometric, physical and visual optics, ocular health assessment, neuroanatomy, ocular anatomy and physiology, pathology, theory and methods of refraction, general and ocular pharmacology, optical and motor aspects of vision, ophthalmic optics, environmental and occupational vision, assessment of oculomotor system, strabismus and vision therapy, visual information processing and perception, ocular disease, contact lenses, pediatric and developmental vision, ethics in health care, professional practice management, low vision and geriatric vision, clinical experience in optometry. **Typical Sequence of High School Courses:** English, algebra, geometry, trigonometry, pre-calculus, biology, computer science, public speaking, chemistry, calculus, physics, foreign language.

Career Snapshot: Optometrists measure patients' visual ability and prescribe visual aids such as glasses and contact lenses. They may evaluate patients' suitability for laser surgery and/or provide post-operative care, but they do not perform surgery. The usual educational preparation is at least three years of college, followed by a four-year program of optometry school. The job outlook is good because the aging population will need increased attention to vision. The best opportunities probably will be at retail vision centers and outpatient clinics.

	Related Job		
Job Title	**Average Earnings**	**Job Growth**	**Job Openings**
Optometrists	$88,290	19.7%	2,000

Characteristics of the Related Job: Interests—Investigative; Realistic; Social. **Skills**—Science; judgment and decision making; management of personnel resources; persuasion; active listening. **Values**—Social service; responsibility; social status; recognition; ability utilization. **Work Conditions**—Exposed to disease or infections; indoors, environmentally controlled; spend time making repetitive motions; using hands on objects, tools, or controls; sitting.

Orthotics/Prosthetics

Prepares individuals, in consultation with physicians and other therapists, to design and fit orthoses for patients with disabling conditions of the limbs and/or spine, and prostheses for patients who have partial or total absence of a limb or significant superficial deformity. **Related CIP Program:** 51.2307 Orthotist/Prosthetist.

Specializations in the Major: Fabrication, fitting, orthotics, prosthetics.

© JIST Works

Typical Sequence of College Courses: English composition, general chemistry, introduction to psychology, general biology, general physics, statistics for business and social sciences, human anatomy and physiology, human growth and development, introduction to computer science, abnormal psychology, kinesiology, fundamentals of medical science, function of the locomotor system, neuroanatomy, lower extremity orthotics, upper extremity orthotics, lower extremity prosthetics, upper extremity prosthetics, psychological aspects of rehabilitation, immediate post-operative and early fitting, spinal orthotics. **Typical Sequence of High School Courses:** English, algebra, geometry, trigonometry, chemistry, physics, biology, art, foreign language, computer science.

Career Snapshot: Orthotics is the design and fitting of supportive or corrective braces for patients with musculoskeletal deformity or injury. Prosthetics is the fabrication and fitting of artificial limbs. People enter this field by getting a bachelor's degree in one or both specializations, or enrolling in a certification program after a bachelor's in another field (perhaps occupational therapy). The job outlook is expected to be good.

Related Jobs			
Job Title	Average Earnings	Job Growth	Job Openings
1. Health Specialties Teachers, Postsecondary	$70,310	32.2%	329,000
2. Medical Appliance Technicians	$28,470	13.2%	1,000
3. Orthotists and Prosthetists	$52,680	18.0%	fewer than 500

Job 1 shares 329,000 job openings with 35 jobs not included in the list.

Characteristics of the Related Jobs: Interests—Investigative; Social; Realistic. **Skills**—Science; instructing; learning strategies; writing; critical thinking. **Values**—Authority; social service; creativity; achievement; social status. **Work Conditions**—Exposed to disease or infections; indoors, environmentally controlled; sitting; exposed to radiation.

Parks and Recreation Management

Prepares individuals to develop and manage park facilities and other indoor and outdoor recreation and leisure facilities. **Related CIP Program:** 31.0301 Parks, Recreation, and Leisure Facilities Management.

Specializations in the Major: Exercise, interpretation, outdoor leadership, resource management, therapeutic recreation, tourism.

Typical Sequence of College Courses: English composition, introduction to computer science, American government, oral communication, conservation of natural resources, introduction to economics, introduction to psychology, statistics for business and social sciences, introduction to sociology, introduction to business management, natural resource economics, ecology, foundations of parks and recreation, tourism management and planning, methods of environmental interpretation, evaluation and research in parks and recreation, parks, recreation and diverse populations, recreation and tourism programs, park planning and design, seminar (reporting on research). **Typical Sequence of High School Courses:** English, biology, social science, chemistry, geometry, public speaking.

Career Snapshot: Interest in the outdoors and in fitness is growing. Americans want to make the most of their recreational time and the parks and other facilities that are set aside for recreational use. Graduates with a bachelor's degree in parks and recreation management may find employment with government, commercial recreational and tourism organizations, camps, or theme parks. However, many people are expected to compete for these jobs, so a master's degree may be an advantage.

Related Job			
Job Title	Average Earnings	Job Growth	Job Openings
Recreation Workers	$19,890	17.3%	69,000

Characteristics of the Related Job: Interest—Social. **Skills**—Management of personnel resources; management of financial resources; service orientation; social perceptiveness; management of material resources. **Values**—Social service; creativity; autonomy; co-workers; authority. **Work Conditions**—Noise levels are distracting or uncomfortable; walking and running; spend time bending or twisting the body; spend time making repetitive motions; very hot or cold.

© JIST Works

Petroleum Engineering

Prepares individuals to apply mathematical and scientific principles to the design, development and operational evaluation of systems for locating, extracting, processing and refining crude petroleum and natural gas. **Related CIP Program:** 14.2501 Petroleum Engineering.

Specializations in the Major: Distribution, drilling/extraction, exploration, refining.

Typical Sequence of College Courses: English composition, introduction to computer science, technical writing, calculus, differential equations, general chemistry, general physics, physical geology, introduction to engineering, statics, dynamics, fluid mechanics, thermodynamics, numerical analysis, materials engineering, engineering economics, heat transfer, sedimentary rocks and processes, petroleum geology, petroleum development, petroleum production methods, petroleum property management, formation evaluation, natural gas engineering, reservoir fluids, reservoir engineering, well testing and analysis, drilling engineering, reservoir stimulation, senior design project. **Typical Sequence of High School Courses:** English, algebra, geometry, trigonometry, pre-calculus, calculus, chemistry, physics, computer science.

Career Snapshot: Petroleum engineers devise technically effective and economically justifiable ways of locating, extracting, transporting, refining, and storing petroleum and natural gas. They apply basic principles of science to oil wells deep in the ground or high-towering refineries. Usually they begin with a bachelor's degree. Management is sometimes an option later in their careers. The job outlook in the United States is favorable and even better in foreign countries.

Related Jobs			
Job Title	Average Earnings	Job Growth	Job Openings
1. Engineering Managers	$99,000	13.0%	15,000
2. Engineering Teachers, Postsecondary	$74,840	32.2%	329,000
3. Petroleum Engineers	$90,040	–0.1%	1,000
Job 2 shares 329,000 job openings with 35 jobs not included in the list.			

Characteristics of the Related Jobs: Interests—Enterprising; Investigative; Realistic. **Skills**—Technology design; science; operations analysis; management of financial resources; mathematics. **Values**—Authority; creativity; autonomy; compensation; ability utilization. **Work Conditions**—Common protective or safety equipment; noise levels are distracting or uncomfortable; sitting; extremely bright or inadequate lighting; hazardous equipment.

Pharmacy

Prepares individuals for the independent or employed practice of preparing and dispensing drugs and medications in consultation with prescribing physicians ad other health care professionals, and for managing pharmacy practices and counseling patients. **Related CIP Program:** 51.2001 Pharmacy (Pharm.D. [USA], Pharm.D. or B.S./B.Pharm. [Canada]).

Specializations in the Major: Pharmaceutical chemistry, pharmacology, pharmacy administration.

Typical Sequence of College Courses: English composition, introduction to psychology, calculus, introduction to sociology, oral communication, general chemistry, general biology, organic chemistry, introduction to biochemistry, human anatomy and physiology, pharmaceutical calculations, pharmacology, pharmaceutics, microbiology and immunology, patient assessment and education, medicinal chemistry, therapeutics, pharmacy law and ethics, pharmacokinetics, electrical inspection. **Typical Sequence of High School Courses:** English, algebra, geometry, trigonometry, biology, computer science, public speaking, chemistry, calculus, physics, foreign language.

Career Snapshot: Pharmacists dispense medications as prescribed by physicians and other health practitioners and give advice to patients about how to use medications. Pharmacists must be knowledgeable about the chemical and physical properties of drugs, how they behave in the body, and how they may interact with other drugs and substances. Schools of pharmacy take about four years to complete and usually require at least one or two years of prior college work. Some pharmacists go on to additional graduate training to prepare for research, administration, or college teaching. Some find work in sales for pharmaceutical companies or in marketing research for managed care organizations. The job outlook for pharmacists is expected to be good, thanks to the aging of the population, combined with the shift of medical care from the scalpel to the pill.

© JIST Works

Related Jobs			
Job Title	Average Earnings	Job Growth	Job Openings
1. Health Specialties Teachers, Postsecondary	$70,310	32.2%	329,000
2. Pharmacists	$87,160	24.6%	16,000

Job 1 shares 329,000 job openings with 35 jobs not included in the list.

Characteristics of the Related Jobs: Interests—Investigative; Conventional; Realistic. **Skills**—Instructing; science; reading comprehension; social perceptiveness; critical thinking. **Values**—Authority; social service; social status; ability utilization; achievement. **Work Conditions**—Exposed to disease or infections; indoors, environmentally controlled; standing; spend time making repetitive motions; specialized protective or safety equipment.

Philosophy

Focuses on ideas and their logical structure, including arguments and investigations about abstract and real phenomena. **Related CIP Program:** 38.0101 Philosophy.

Specializations in the Major: Esthetics, ethics, history of philosophy, logic.

Typical Sequence of College Courses: English composition, foreign language, introduction to logic, major thinkers and issues in philosophy, ethical/moral theory, classical philosophy, modern philosophy, contemporary philosophy, esthetics. **Typical Sequence of High School Courses:** Algebra, English, foreign language, social science, history, geometry.

Career Snapshot: Philosophy is concerned with the most basic questions about the human experience, such as what reality is, what the ultimate values are, and how we know what we know. Philosophy majors are trained to think independently and critically, and to write clearly and persuasively. They may go to work in a number of business careers where these skills are appreciated—perhaps most of all in the long run as these former philosophy majors advance to positions of leadership. Some find that a philosophy major combines well with further training in law, computer science, or religious studies. Those with a graduate degree in philosophy may teach in college.

Related Job			
Job Title	Average Earnings	Job Growth	Job Openings
Philosophy and Religion Teachers, Postsecondary	$52,580	32.2%	329,000

This job shares 329,000 job openings with 35 jobs not included in the list.

Characteristics of the Related Job: Interest—Social. **Skills**—Service orientation; social perceptiveness; writing; speaking; reading comprehension. **Values**—Social service; social status; autonomy; achievement; recognition. **Work Conditions**—Indoors, environmentally controlled; sitting.

Physical Education

Prepares individuals to teach physical education programs and/or to coach sports at various educational levels. **Related CIP Program:** 13.1314 Physical Education Teaching and Coaching.

Specializations in the Major: Coaching, health education, recreation, sports activities.

Typical Sequence of College Courses: Introduction to psychology, English composition, oral communication, history and philosophy of education, human growth and development, introduction to special education, history and philosophy of physical education, first aid and CPR, methods of teaching physical education, human anatomy and physiology, kinesiology, special needs in physical education, psychomotor development, organization and administration of physical ed., evaluation in physical education, methods of teaching dance, methods of teaching sports activities, methods of teaching aerobics and weight training, swimming and water safety, student teaching. **Typical Sequence of High School Courses:** English, algebra, geometry, trigonometry, science, foreign language, public speaking.

Career Snapshot: This major covers not only educational techniques, but also the workings of the human body. Thanks to a national concern for fitness and health, physical education graduates are finding employment not only as teachers, but also as instructors and athletic directors in health and sports clubs. Most jobs are still to be found in elementary and secondary schools, where a bachelor's degree is often sufficient for entry, but a master's may be required for advancement to a more secure and better-paid

© JIST Works

position. Some graduates may go on to get a master's in athletic training and work for a college or professional sports team.

Related Jobs			
Job Title	Average Earnings	Job Growth	Job Openings
1. Coaches and Scouts	$25,930	20.4%	63,000
2. Education Teachers, Postsecondary	$50,410	32.2%	329,000
3. Fitness Trainers and Aerobics Instructors	$26,070	27.1%	50,000
4. Middle School Teachers, Except Special and Vocational Education	$44,180	13.7%	83,000
5. Secondary School Teachers, Except Special and Vocational Education	$46,120	14.4%	107,000

Job 2 shares 329,000 job openings with 35 jobs not included in the list.

Characteristics of the Related Jobs: Interest—Social. **Skills**—Instructing; learning strategies; social perceptiveness; persuasion; monitoring. **Values**—Authority; social service; creativity; responsibility; achievement. **Work Conditions**—Standing; noise levels are distracting or uncomfortable; walking and running; indoors, environmentally controlled.

Physical Therapy

Prepares individuals to alleviate physical and functional impairments and limitations caused by injury or disease through the design and implementation of therapeutic interventions to promote fitness and health. **Related CIP Program:** 51.2308 Physical Therapy/Therapist.

Specializations in the Major: Geriatric physical therapy, neurological physical therapy, orthopedics, physical therapy education, sports medicine.

Typical Sequence of College Courses: English composition, statistics for business and social sciences, general chemistry, general biology, human anatomy and physiology, introduction to psychology, human growth and development, introduction to computer science, abnormal psychology, fundamentals of medical science, neuroanatomy, neuroscience for therapy, cardiopulmonary system, musculoskeletal system, clinical orthopedics, clinical applications of neurophysiology, therapeutic exercise techniques, physical and electrical agents in physical therapy, medical considerations in physical therapy, psychomotor development throughout the lifespan, psychosocial aspects of physical disability, research in physical therapy practice, research in physical therapy practice. **Typical Sequence of High School Courses:** English, algebra, geometry, trigonometry, chemistry, physics, biology, foreign language, computer science.

Career Snapshot: Physical therapists help people overcome pain and limited movement caused by disease or injury, and help them avoid further disabilities. They review patients' medical records and the prescriptions of physicians, evaluate patients' mobility, then guide patients through appropriate exercise routines and apply therapeutic agents such as heat and electrical stimulation. They need to be knowledgeable about many disabling conditions and therapeutic techniques. The master's program is becoming the standard requirement for entry into this field. Entry to master's programs is extremely competitive. The short-term job outlook has been hurt by cutbacks in Medicare coverage of therapy; however, the long-term outlook is expected to be good.

Related Jobs			
Job Title	*Average Earnings*	*Job Growth*	*Job Openings*
1. Health Specialties Teachers, Postsecondary	$70,310	32.2%	329,000
2. Physical Therapists	$61,560	36.7%	13,000

Job 1 shares 329,000 job openings with 35 jobs not included in the list.

Characteristics of the Related Jobs: Interests—Social; Investigative; Realistic. **Skills**—Science; instructing; learning strategies; reading comprehension; time management. **Values**—Social service; authority; achievement; ability utilization; co-workers. **Work Conditions**—Exposed to disease or infections; indoors, environmentally controlled; specialized protective or safety equipment; cramped work space, awkward positions; spend time keeping or regaining balance.

Physician Assisting

Prepares individuals to practice medicine, including diagnoses and treatment therapies, under the supervision of a physician. **Related CIP Program:** 51.0912 Physician Assistant.

Specializations in the Major: Emergency medicine, family medicine, internal medicine, pediatrics.

Typical Sequence of College Courses: English composition, college algebra, general chemistry, general biology, introduction to psychology, human growth and development, general microbiology, human physiology, human anatomy, pharmacology, medical interviewing techniques, patient examination and evaluation, clinical laboratory procedures, ethics in health care, clinical experience in internal medicine, clinical experience in emergency medicine, clinical experience in obstetrics/gynecology, clinical experience in family medicine, clinical experience in psychiatry, clinical experience in surgery, clinical experience in pediatrics, clinical experience in geriatrics.

Typical Sequence of High School Courses: English, algebra, geometry, trigonometry, pre-calculus, biology, computer science, public speaking, chemistry, foreign language.

Career Snapshot: Physician assistants work under the supervision of physicians, but in some cases they provide care in settings where a physician may be present only a couple of days per week. They perform many of the diagnostic, therapeutic, and preventative functions that we are used to associating with physicians. The typical educational program results in a bachelor's degree. It often takes only two years to complete, but entrants usually must have at least two years of prior college and often must have work experience in the field of health care. Employment opportunities are expected to be good.

Related Jobs			
Job Title	Average Earnings	Job Growth	Job Openings
1. Health Specialties Teachers, Postsecondary	$70,310	32.2%	329,000
2. Physician Assistants	$69,250	49.6%	10,000

Job 1 shares 329,000 job openings with 35 jobs not included in the list.

Characteristics of the Related Jobs: Interests—Investigative; Social; Artistic. Skills—Science; instructing; critical thinking; writing; reading comprehension. Values—Social service; authority; achievement; ability utilization; social status. Work Conditions—Exposed to disease or infections; indoors, environmentally controlled; exposed to radiation; sitting; specialized protective or safety equipment.

Physics

Focuses on the scientific study of matter and energy, and the formulation and testing of the laws governing the behavior of the matter-energy continuum. Related CIP Program: 40.0801 Physics, General.

Specializations in the Major: Acoustics, astronomy, elementary particles, nuclear physics, optics, plasma physics, solid-state physics, theoretical physics.

Typical Sequence of College Courses: English composition, introduction to computer science, calculus, differential equations, general chemistry, mechanics, optics, thermal physics, electricity and magnetism, modern physics, modern experimental physics, quantum and atomic physics. Typical Sequence of High School Courses: English, algebra, geometry, trigonometry, chemistry, physics, pre-calculus, computer science, calculus.

Career Snapshot: Physics is the study of the basic laws of the physical world, including those that govern what matter and energy are and how they change form, move, and interact. This knowledge is the basis for our understanding of many fields, such as chemistry, biology, and engineering. Physics has direct applications in the technologies that we use every day for transportation, communication, and entertainment. For jobs in basic research and development, as well as for college teaching, a Ph.D. is most commonly required. Unfortunately, research is not expected to grow fast, if at all, so there will be keen competition for jobs as physicists. Job opportunities will be better for physics graduates in applied settings, where they do work associated with engineering and computer science. High school teaching is also an option. Most states require that new teachers eventually get a master's degree.

© JIST Works

Related Jobs			
Job Title	Average Earnings	Job Growth	Job Openings
1. Natural Sciences Managers	$90,080	13.6%	5,000
2. Physicists	$87,480	7.0%	1,000
3. Physics Teachers, Postsecondary	$65,280	32.2%	329,000

Job 3 shares 329,000 job openings with 35 jobs not included in the list.

Characteristics of the Related Jobs: Interests—Investigative; Realistic; Enterprising. **Skills**—Science; mathematics; active learning; writing; critical thinking. **Values**—Creativity; authority; autonomy; working conditions; ability utilization. **Work Conditions**—Indoors, environmentally controlled; sitting; hazardous conditions; specialized protective or safety equipment.

Podiatry

Prepares individuals for the independent professional practice of podiatric medicine, involving the prevention, diagnosis, and treatment of diseases, disorders, and injuries to the foot and lower extremities. **Related CIP Program:** 51.2101 Podiatric Medicine/Podiatry (D.P.M.).

Specializations in the Major: Orthopedics, sports medicine, surgery.

Typical Sequence of College Courses: English composition, introduction to psychology, college algebra, calculus, introduction to sociology, oral communication, general chemistry, general biology, introduction to computer science, organic chemistry, human anatomy and physiology, general microbiology, genetics, introduction to biochemistry, gross anatomy, histology, patient examination and evaluation, lower extremity anatomy, neuroanatomy, human physiology, microbiology and immunology, pathology, biomechanics, radiology, podiatric surgery, dermatology, general medicine, traumatology, professional practice management, clinical experience in podiatric medicine. **Typical Sequence of High School Courses:** English, algebra, geometry, trigonometry, biology, computer science, public speaking, chemistry, foreign language, physics, pre-calculus.

Career Snapshot: Podiatrists are health care practitioners who specialize in the feet and lower extremities. The educational process is much like that for medical doctors—for almost all students, first a bachelor's degree, then four years of study and clinical practice in a school of podiatric medicine, followed by one to three years of a hospital residency program. The bachelor's degree can be in any subject as long as it includes certain coursework in science and math. Job opportunities will probably be better in group medical practices, clinics, and health networks than in traditional solo practices.

Related Job			
Job Title	**Average Earnings**	**Job Growth**	**Job Openings**
Podiatrists	$97,290	16.2%	1,000

Characteristics of the Related Job: Interests—Social; Investigative; Enterprising. **Skills**—Science; active listening; complex problem solving; management of financial resources; reading comprehension. **Values**—Social service; responsibility; recognition; autonomy; social status. **Work Conditions**—Exposed to disease or infections; exposed to radiation; common protective or safety equipment; specialized protective or safety equipment; contaminants.

Political Science

Focuses on the systematic study of political institutions and behavior. **Related CIP Program:** 45.1001 Political Science and Government, General.

Specializations in the Major: Comparative politics, international relations, political theory, public administration, public opinion, public policy.

Typical Sequence of College Courses: English composition, introduction to psychology, introduction to sociology, American government, foreign language, statistics, introduction to economics, statistics for business and social sciences, state and local government, comparative governments, introduction to international relations, political theory, political science research methods, public policy analysis, seminar (reporting on research). **Typical Sequence of High School Courses:** Algebra, English, foreign language, social science, trigonometry, history.

Career Snapshot: Political science is the study of how political systems and public policy are created and evolve. It is concerned with many levels of political activity, from the campaigns of candidates for representation of a city precinct to the maneuvers of nations trying to resolve regional conflicts. Most political scientists with graduate degrees work as researchers and teachers in universities; some work for nonprofits, political lobbyists, and social organizations. Many holders of the bachelor's degree use it as an entry route to law school or public administration.

Related Jobs			
Job Title	Average Earnings	Job Growth	Job Openings
1. Political Science Teachers, Postsecondary	$59,530	32.2%	329,000
2. Political Scientists	$86,460	7.3%	fewer than 500

Job 1 shares 329,000 job openings with 35 jobs not included in the list.

Characteristics of the Related Jobs: Interests—Investigative; Social; Artistic. **Skills**—Instructing; writing; persuasion; critical thinking; reading comprehension. **Values**—Authority; creativity; autonomy; social service; responsibility. **Work Conditions**—Sitting; indoors, environmentally controlled.

Psychology

Focuses on the scientific study of individual and collective behavior, the physical and environmental bases of behavior, and the analysis and treatment of behavior problems and disorders. **Related CIP Program:** 42.0101 Psychology, General.

Specializations in the Major: Clinical/counseling psychology, educational psychology, industrial psychology, research clinical psychology.

Typical Sequence of College Courses: Introduction to psychology, English composition, statistics, research methods in speech pathology and audiology, experimental psychology, psychology of learning, abnormal psychology, social psychology, developmental psychology, sensation and perception, cognitive psychology, biopsychology, psychology of personality, quantitative analysis in psychology, psychological testing and measurements. **Typical**

Sequence of High School Courses: Algebra, biology, English, foreign language, social science, trigonometry.

Career Snapshot: Psychology is the study of human behavior. It may take place in a clinical, educational, industrial, or experimental setting. Those with a bachelor's degree usually must find employment in another field, such as marketing research. A bachelor's degree can also be a good first step toward graduate education in education, law, social work, or another field. To be licensed as a clinical or counseling psychologist, you usually need a Ph.D. Industrial-organizational psychologists need a master's. School psychologists need an educational specialist degree and may enjoy the best job opportunities in this field. Competition for graduate school is expected to be keen. About half of psychologists are self-employed. Because psychology is about behavior, many people don't realize that it uses scientific methods and that students are expected to become competent in statistics.

Related Jobs			
Job Title	**Average Earnings**	**Job Growth**	**Job Openings**
1. Clinical Psychologists	$56,360	19.1%	10,000
2. Counseling Psychologists	$56,360	19.1%	10,000
3. Educational Psychologists	$56,360	19.1%	10,000
4. Industrial-Organizational Psychologists	$74,060	20.4%	fewer than 500
5. Psychology Teachers, Postsecondary	$55,750	32.2%	329,000

Jobs 1, 2, and 3 share 10,000 job openings. Job 5 shares 329,000 job openings with 35 jobs not included in the list.

Characteristics of the Related Jobs: Interests—Investigative; Social; Artistic. **Skills**—Social perceptiveness; active listening; persuasion; learning strategies; reading comprehension. **Values**—Social service; creativity; autonomy; ability utilization; responsibility. **Work Conditions**—Sitting; indoors, environmentally controlled.

Public Administration

Prepares individuals to serve as managers in the executive arm of local, state, and federal government; and that focuses on the systematic study of

© JIST Works

executive organization and management. **Related CIP Program:** 44.0401 Public Administration.

Specializations in the Major: Economic development, finance and budgeting, personnel and labor relations, policy analysis, program management.

Typical Sequence of College Courses: English composition, oral communication, accounting, introduction to business management, American government, state and local government, college algebra, introduction to economics, organizational behavior, statistics for business and social sciences, organizational theory, introduction to psychology, urban politics, public policy making process, public finance and budgeting, political science research methods, planning and change in public organizations, seminar (reporting on research). **Typical Sequence of High School Courses:** Algebra, English, foreign language, social science, trigonometry, history, public speaking, computer science.

Career Snapshot: The public sector includes many kinds of agencies, working in the fields of health, law enforcement, environmental protection, transportation, and taxation, to name just a few. Because of this variety of fields, graduates who have been trained in administrative skills (perhaps at the master's level) often find it helpful to combine that background with specific training in another field, such as health, science, engineering, or accounting. Public administration programs usually include internships that give students actual experience working in a public agency.

Related Jobs			
Job Title	Average Earnings	Job Growth	Job Openings
1. Administrative Services Managers	$62,300	16.9%	25,000
2. Chief Executives	$141,820	14.9%	38,000
3. Emergency Management Specialists	$45,670	22.8%	2,000
4. General and Operations Managers	$79,300	17.0%	208,000
5. Government Service Executives	$141,820	14.9%	38,000

(continued)

(continued)

Job Title	Average Earnings	Job Growth	Job Openings
6. Postmasters and Mail Superintendents	$50,520	0.0%	2,000
7. Social and Community Service Managers	$48,330	25.5%	17,000
8. Storage and Distribution Managers	$67,300	12.7%	15,000
9. Transportation Managers	$67,300	12.7%	15,000

Job 5 shares 38,000 job openings with another job not included in the list. Jobs 8 and 9 share 15,000 job openings.

Characteristics of the Related Jobs: Interests—Enterprising; Conventional; Social. **Skills**—Management of financial resources; management of personnel resources; management of material resources; negotiation; monitoring. **Values**—Authority; autonomy; creativity; responsibility; social status. **Work Conditions**—Walking and running; indoors, environmentally controlled; sitting; outdoors, exposed to weather.

Public Relations

Focuses on the theories and methods for managing the media image of a business, organization, or individual and the communication process with stakeholders, constituencies, audiences, and the general public; and that prepares individuals to function as public relations assistants, technicians, and managers. **Related CIP Program:** 09.0902 Public Relations/Image Management.

Specializations in the Major: Creative process, management, new media.

Typical Sequence of College Courses: English composition, oral communication, introduction to marketing, introduction to economics, principles of public relations, communications theory, public relations message strategy, communication ethics, public relations media, public relations writing, public relations techniques and campaigns, organizational communications, mass communication law, introduction to communication research, visual design for media. **Typical Sequence of High School Courses:** English, algebra, foreign language, art, literature, public speaking, social science.

© JIST Works

Career Snapshot: Public relations specialists work for business, government, and nonprofit organizations and encourage public support for the employer's policies and practices. Often several "publics" with differing interests and needs have to be targeted with different messages. The work requires understanding of psychology, the business and social environments, effective writing, and techniques used in various media for persuasive communications. A bachelor's degree is good preparation for an entry-level job in this competitive field, and an internship or work experience is an important advantage. On-the-job experience may lead to a job managing public relations campaigns; a master's degree can speed up the process of advancement.

Related Jobs			
Job Title	Average Earnings	Job Growth	Job Openings
1. Advertising and Promotions Managers	$66,560	20.3%	9,000
2. Communications Teachers, Postsecondary	$50,610	32.2%	329,000
3. Public Relations Managers	$73,960	21.7%	5,000
4. Public Relations Specialists	$44,390	22.9%	38,000

Job 2 shares 329,000 job openings with 35 jobs not included in the list.

Characteristics of the Related Jobs: Interests—Enterprising; Artistic; Social. **Skills**—Service orientation; persuasion; management of financial resources; negotiation; coordination. **Values**—Creativity; recognition; authority; ability utilization; achievement. **Work Conditions**—Sitting.

Religion/Religious Studies

Prepares individuals for ordination as ministers or priests in any of the Christian religious traditions. 38.0201 Religion/Religious Studies focuses on the nature of religious belief and specific religious and quasi-religious systems. **Related CIP Programs:** 39.0602 Divinity/Ministry (B.D., M.Div.); 38.0201 Religion/Religious Studies.

Specializations in the Major: Ecumenical studies, missionary work, pastoral counseling, pastoral studies, scriptural texts/language.

Typical Sequence of College Courses: English composition, foreign language, introduction to religious studies, introduction to philosophy, ethical/moral theory, Hebrew Bible, New Testament, non-Western religions, philosophy of religion, history of religion in the West, contemporary theologies, religious ethics. **Typical Sequence of High School Courses:** Algebra, English, foreign language, social science, history, geometry, public speaking.

Career Snapshot: Interest in religion continues to grow in America, and many colleges were founded by churches, so the religious studies major continues to attract students, some of whom do not feel the call to become professional clergy. A graduate of a religious studies major has skills in language, literature, critical thinking, and writing that are valuable in many careers in the secular world. The amount of education required to be ordained in the clergy depends on the person's religious denomination. For some, there may be no formal requirement; most require several years of seminary training, often following four years of college. Clergy find work in churches, synagogues, and religious schools; as chaplains for hospitals, prisons, and the military; and as missionaries.

Related Jobs			
Job Title	Average Earnings	Job Growth	Job Openings
1. Clergy	$37,870	12.4%	26,000
2. Philosophy and Religion Teachers, Postsecondary	$52,580	32.2%	329,000

Job 2 shares 329,000 job openings with 35 jobs not included in the list.

Characteristics of the Related Jobs: Interest—Social. **Skills**—Service orientation; social perceptiveness; writing; speaking; reading comprehension. **Values**—Social service; social status; autonomy; achievement; recognition. **Work Conditions**—Indoors, environmentally controlled; sitting.

Russian

Focuses on the Russian language; includes the cultural and historical contexts, dialects, and applications to business, science/technology, and other settings. **Related CIP Program:** 16.0402 Russian Language and Literature.

© JIST Works

Specializations in the Major: History and culture, language education, literature, translation.

Typical Sequence of College Courses: Russian language, conversation, composition, linguistics, Russian literature, Russian history and civilization, European history and civilization, grammar, phonetics. **Typical Sequence of High School Courses:** English, public speaking, foreign language, history, literature, social science.

Career Snapshot: Despite the breakup of the Soviet Union, Russian is still an important world language that not many Americans know. As business and governmental ties with Russia continue to increase as it opens to free trade, a degree in Russian can lead to careers in international business, travel, and law. College teaching and translation are options for those with a graduate degree in Russian.

Related Jobs			
Job Title	*Average Earnings*	*Job Growth*	*Job Openings*
1. Foreign Language and Literature Teachers, Postsecondary	$49,120	32.2%	329,000
2. Interpreters and Translators	$34,900	19.9%	4,000

Job 1 shares 329,000 job openings with 35 jobs not included in the list.

Characteristics of the Related Jobs: Interests—Artistic; Social; Investigative. **Skills**—Writing; active listening; speaking; reading comprehension; service orientation. **Values**—Social service; ability utilization; achievement; autonomy; social status. **Work Conditions**—Sitting; indoors, environmentally controlled.

Secondary Education

Prepares individuals to teach students in the secondary grades, which may include grades seven through twelve, depending on the school system or state regulations. May include preparation to teach a comprehensive curriculum or specific subject matter. **Related CIP Program:** 13.1205 Secondary Education and Teaching.

Specializations in the Major: Art education, bilingual education, language education, mathematics education, music education, remedial and developmental reading, science education, social studies education.

Typical Sequence of College Courses: Introduction to psychology, English composition, oral communication, history and philosophy of education, human growth and development, teaching methods, educational alternatives for exceptional students, educational psychology, courses in subject to be taught, student teaching. **Typical Sequence of High School Courses:** English, algebra, geometry, trigonometry, science, foreign language, public speaking.

Career Snapshot: A bachelor's is the minimum for starting a secondary teaching career, and a master's may be required or encouraged for job security and a pay raise. A teacher-education program covers not only the subjects you will teach, but also basic principles of how young people learn and how to run a classroom. Demand for secondary school teachers is expected to be better than that for lower grades, but it will vary according to subject field and geographic area. Job opportunities will be best in inner-city and rural locations.

Related Job			
Job Title	Average Earnings	Job Growth	Job Openings
Secondary School Teachers, Except Special and Vocational Education	$46,120	14.4%	107,000

Characteristics of the Related Job: Interest—Social. **Skills**—Learning strategies; instructing; persuasion; social perceptiveness; monitoring. **Values**—Social service; authority; creativity; responsibility; achievement. **Work Conditions**—Standing; noise levels are distracting or uncomfortable; indoors, environmentally controlled; contaminants.

Social Work

Prepares individuals for the professional practice of social welfare administration and counseling, and that focus on the study of organized means of providing basic support services for vulnerable individuals and groups. **Related CIP Program:** 44.0701 Social Work.

Specializations in the Major: Advocacy, child welfare, domestic violence, health care, mental health, mental retardation, school, substance abuse.

Typical Sequence of College Courses: English composition, human growth and development, American government, introduction to psychology, introduction to sociology, introduction to philosophy, statistics for business and social sciences, cultural diversity, human anatomy and physiology, development of social welfare, human behavior and the social environment, social work methods, social welfare policy and issues, field experience/internship, social work research methods, foreign language, seminar (reporting on research). **Typical Sequence of High School Courses:** Algebra, biology, English, foreign language, social science, trigonometry.

Career Snapshot: Social workers improve people's lives by helping them cope with problems of bad health, substance abuse, disability, old age, family conflicts, mental illness, or poverty. A large number of them work for public agencies and health care institutions. A master's degree is becoming standard preparation for this field. Job opportunities are expected to be best in rural areas and in the specializations of substance abuse and gerontology.

Related Jobs			
Job Title	*Average Earnings*	*Job Growth*	*Job Openings*
1. Child, Family, and School Social Workers	$35,010	19.0%	31,000
2. Marriage and Family Therapists	$40,440	25.4%	3,000
3. Probation Officers and Correctional Treatment Specialists	$39,760	12.8%	14,000
4. Social Work Teachers, Postsecondary	$52,160	32.2%	329,000

Job 4 shares 329,000 job openings with 35 jobs not included in the list.

Characteristics of the Related Jobs: Interest—Social. **Skills**—Social perceptiveness; service orientation; persuasion; negotiation; learning strategies. **Values**—Social service; autonomy; authority; activity; variety. **Work**

Conditions—Exposed to disease or infections; outdoors, exposed to weather; sitting; noise levels are distracting or uncomfortable; very hot or cold.

Sociology

Focuses on the systematic study of human social institutions and social relationships. **Related CIP Program:** 45.1101 Sociology.

Specializations in the Major: Anthropology, criminology, culture and social change, family and marriage, gerontology, human relations, social institutions/organizations, social problems.

Typical Sequence of College Courses: English composition, introduction to psychology, introduction to sociology, American government, introduction to economics, statistics, foreign language, social inequality, introduction to social research, history of social thought, contemporary social problems, seminar (reporting on research). **Typical Sequence of High School Courses:** Algebra, English, foreign language, social science, trigonometry.

Career Snapshot: Sociologists study how people behave within groups, such as families, religious denominations, social organizations, businesses, and political groups. Many graduates of bachelor's sociology programs go on to graduate school with the goal of research or teaching. Others branch out to a related field, perhaps with additional education, such as social work, the law, or marketing research.

Related Jobs			
Job Title	Average Earnings	Job Growth	Job Openings
1. Sociologists	$56,790	4.7%	fewer than 500
2. Sociology Teachers, Postsecondary	$54,600	32.2%	329,000
Job 2 shares 329,000 job openings with 35 jobs not included in the list.			

Characteristics of the Related Jobs: Interests—Social; Investigative; Artistic. **Skills**—Instructing; learning strategies; writing; social perceptiveness; science. **Values**—Authority; creativity; social service; responsibility; autonomy. **Work Conditions**—Indoors, environmentally controlled; sitting.

© JIST Works

Soil Science

Focuses on the scientific classification of soils, soil properties, and their relationship to agricultural crops. **Related CIP Programs:** 01.1202 Soil Chemistry and Physics; 01.1203 Soil Microbiology; 01.1201 Soil Science and Agronomy, General.

Specializations in the Major: Land-use management, soil conservation, soil surveying, sustainable agriculture, waste/bioresource management.

Typical Sequence of College Courses: English composition, calculus, general biology, general chemistry, organic chemistry, general physics, introduction to geology, introduction to soil science, statistics, computer applications in agriculture, soil mechanics, soil chemistry, soil conservation engineering, soil morphology, soil analysis, soil fertility, ecology, introduction to ground water/hydrology, natural resource management and water quality, ecology and renewable resource management. **Typical Sequence of High School Courses:** Biology, chemistry, algebra, geometry, trigonometry, computer science, English, public speaking.

Career Snapshot: Soil is a lot more than just dirt. It is a complex ecosystem with chemical, physical, mineralogical, and biological properties that affect agricultural productivity and the larger environment. Soil scientists survey and map soils, advise farmers and landowners on how to use land in productive and ecologically sound methods, and consult with civil engineers about construction projects that involve soil. Many work for governments; the federal government hires graduates of bachelor's degree programs. Those with advanced degrees may go into college teaching or basic research.

Related Jobs			
Job Title	Average Earnings	Job Growth	Job Openings
1. Agricultural Sciences Teachers, Postsecondary	$70,610	32.2%	329,000
2. Biochemists	$68,700	21.0%	1,000
3. Biophysicists	$68,700	21.0%	1,000
4. Microbiologists	$55,300	17.2%	1,000
5. Soil Scientists	$53,240	13.9%	1,000

Job 1 shares 329,000 job openings with 35 jobs not included in the list. Jobs 2 and 3 share 1,000 job openings.

Characteristics of the Related Jobs: Interests—Investigative; Realistic; Conventional. **Skills**—Science; writing; reading comprehension; active learning; mathematics. **Values**—Creativity; autonomy; ability utilization; responsibility; social status. **Work Conditions**—Exposed to disease or infections; indoors, environmentally controlled; common protective or safety equipment; exposed to radiation; hazardous conditions.

Spanish

Focuses on the Spanish language and related dialects; includes the cultural and historical contexts and applications to business, science/technology, and other settings. **Related CIP Program:** 16.0905 Spanish Language and Literature.

Specializations in the Major: History and culture, language education, literature, translation.

Typical Sequence of College Courses: Spanish language, conversation, composition, linguistics, Spanish literature, Spanish-American literature, Spanish history and civilization, European history and civilization, grammar, phonetics. **Typical Sequence of High School Courses:** English, public speaking, Spanish, history, literature, social science.

Career Snapshot: Spanish has become the second language in the United States, as well as maintaining its importance as a world language, especially in the Western Hemisphere. A degree in Spanish can be useful preparation (perhaps with an additional degree) for many careers in business, travel, and public service, and not just with an international orientation. High school teaching usually requires a master's degree for security and advancement.

Related Jobs			
Job Title	*Average Earnings*	*Job Growth*	*Job Openings*
1. Foreign Language and Literature Teachers, Postsecondary	$49,120	32.2%	329,000
2. Interpreters and Translators	$34,900	19.9%	4,000
Job 1 shares 329,000 job openings with 35 jobs not included in the list.			

© JIST Works

Characteristics of the Related Jobs: Interests—Artistic; Social; Investigative. **Skills**—Writing; active listening; speaking; reading comprehension; service orientation. **Values**—Social service; ability utilization; achievement; autonomy; social status. **Work Conditions**—Sitting; indoors, environmentally controlled.

Special Education

Focuses on the design and provision of teaching and other educational services to children or adults with special learning needs or disabilities, and that may prepare individuals to function as special education teachers. **Related CIP Program:** 13.1001 Special Education and Teaching, General.

Specializations in the Major: Autism, multiple disabilities, specific learning disabilities, speech-language impairments, traumatic brain injury, visual impairments.

Typical Sequence of College Courses: Introduction to psychology, English composition, oral communication, history and philosophy of education, human growth and development, introduction to special education, curriculum and methods for special education, educational psychology, psychology of the exceptional child, assessment in special education, classroom/laboratory management, behavior modification techniques in education, education for moderate and severe disabilities, reading assessment and teaching, mathematics education, student teaching. **Typical Sequence of High School Courses:** English, algebra, geometry, trigonometry, science, foreign language, public speaking.

Career Snapshot: Special education covers a wide variety of learning and developmental disabilities and other conditions that require nonstandard educational techniques. Many states require a master's degree for licensure, but some states are offering alternative entry routes. Job opportunity in this field is excellent, especially in rural areas and inner cities, and for specializations such as multiple disabilities, autism, and bilingual special education.

Related Jobs			
Job Title	Average Earnings	Job Growth	Job Openings
1. Special Education Teachers, Middle School	$45,000	19.9%	8,000
2. Special Education Teachers, Preschool, Kindergarten, and Elementary School	$44,330	23.3%	18,000
3. Special Education Teachers, Secondary School	$46,300	17.9%	11,000

Characteristics of the Related Jobs: Interest—Social. **Skills**—Learning strategies; instructing; social perceptiveness; negotiation; time management. **Values**—Social service; authority; creativity; achievement; responsibility. **Work Conditions**—Exposed to disease or infections; noise levels are distracting or uncomfortable; standing.

Speech-Language Pathology and Audiology

Integrates or coordinates several subjects to prepare individuals as audiologists and speech-language pathologists. **Related CIP Program:** 51.0204 Audiology/Audiologist and Speech-Language Pathology/Pathologist.

Specializations in the Major: Audiology, speech-language pathology.

Typical Sequence of College Courses: General biology, English composition, general physics, introduction to psychology, human growth and development, statistics, introduction to sociology, introduction to speech, language and hearing, phonetics, anatomy of the speech and hearing mechanism, linguistics, psychoacoustics, neuroscience, auditory anatomy and physiology, stuttering and other fluency disorders, voice disorders, hearing problems, psycholinguistics and speech perception, diagnostic procedures in audiology, aural rehabilitation, research methods in speech pathology and audiology, student teaching. **Typical Sequence of High School Courses:** English, algebra, geometry, trigonometry, biology, chemistry, physics, computer science, public speaking, social science, pre-calculus.

© JIST Works

Career Snapshot: Speech-language pathologists and audiologists help people with a variety of communication disorders. About half of speech-language pathologists work in schools, most of the rest for health care facilities. Among audiologists, about half work in health care settings, with a smaller number in schools. A master's degree is the standard entry route for speech-language pathologists. For audiologists, a master's still suffices in many states ,but a doctoral degree is expected to become the standard. It is possible to complete the requirements for entering both kinds of graduate program within a variety of undergraduate majors. Because of the aging of the population and an emphasis on early diagnosis, job opportunities are expected to be excellent for speech-language pathologists, though less certain for audiologists. Knowledge of a second language is an advantage.

Related Jobs			
Job Title	*Average Earnings*	*Job Growth*	*Job Openings*
1. Audiologists	$53,040	9.1%	fewer than 500
2. Health Specialties Teachers, Postsecondary	$70,310	32.2%	329,000
3. Speech-Language Pathologists	$53,790	14.6%	5,000

Job 2 shares 329,000 job openings with 35 jobs not included in the list.

Characteristics of the Related Jobs: Interests—Investigative; Social. **Skills**—Instructing; learning strategies; science; active learning; time management. **Values**—Social service; authority; creativity; achievement; ability utilization. **Work Conditions**—Exposed to disease or infections; sitting; indoors, environmentally controlled.

Statistics

Focuses on the relationships between groups of measurements, and similarities and differences, using probability theory and techniques derived from it. **Related CIP Programs:** 27.0502 Mathematical Statistics and Probability; 27.0501 Statistics, General.

Specializations in the Major: Computer applications, experimental design, mathematical statistics, probability, psychometrics.

Typical Sequence of College Courses: Calculus, introduction to computer science, programming in a language (e.g., C, PASCAL, COBOL), statistics, linear algebra, experimental design and analysis, mathematical statistics, seminar (reporting on research). **Typical Sequence of High School Courses:** Algebra, geometry, trigonometry, pre-calculus, calculus, computer science, physics.

Career Snapshot: Statistical analysis is a valuable tool that is used by every discipline that deals in quantitative information—social sciences, laboratory sciences, and business studies. Statisticians find meaningful patterns in data sets that are harvested from experiments, surveys, and other procedures such as bookkeeping. Graduates of statistics programs are in demand in many parts of the economy, from basic research to business management, from government to academia. Some get advanced degrees to specialize in research or college teaching, or get a degree in a second field such as psychology, computer science, or business.

Related Jobs			
Job Title	**Average Earnings**	**Job Growth**	**Job Openings**
1. Mathematical Science Teachers, Postsecondary	$53,250	32.2%	329,000
2. Mathematicians	$81,010	−1.3%	fewer than 500
3. Natural Sciences Managers	$90,080	13.6%	5,000
4. Statisticians	$59,960	4.6%	2,000

Job 1 shares 329,000 job openings with 35 jobs not included in the list.

Characteristics of the Related Jobs: Interests—Investigative; Conventional; Realistic. **Skills**—Mathematics; science; active learning; critical thinking; complex problem solving. **Values**—Authority; creativity; autonomy; ability utilization; working conditions. **Work Conditions**—Indoors, environmentally controlled; sitting.

Transportation and Logistics Management

Prepares individuals to plan, administer, and coordinate physical transportation operations, networks, and systems or to manage and coordinate all logistical functions in an enterprise. **Related CIP Programs:** 52.0203 Logistics and Materials Management; 52.0209 Transportation/ Transportation Management.

Specializations in the Major: Inventory control, location analysis, management information systems, materials handling, order fulfillment, planning and forecasting, traffic and transportation management, warehouse operations.

Typical Sequence of College Courses: English composition, business writing, introduction to psychology, principles of microeconomics, principles of macroeconomics, calculus for business and social sciences, statistics for business and social sciences, introduction to management information systems, introduction to accounting, legal environment of business, business finance, introduction to marketing, human resource management, introduction to logistics, transportation management, inventory management, analysis and design of logistics systems. **Typical Sequence of High School Courses:** English, algebra, geometry, trigonometry, foreign language, computer science, public speaking, pre-calculus.

Career Snapshot: Transportation and logistics managers find the fastest and most cost-effective ways to keep materials flowing through our economy. Any business that produces goods or uses supplies—and that means practically every business—faces problems that these specialists are trained to solve. Some enter the field with a bachelor's in transportation and logistics management. On-the-job experience is important for advancement. Those interested in a technical specialization such as inventory control, packaging, or forecasting may major in (or get a master's degree in) management information systems, operations research, or industrial engineering.

Related Jobs			
Job Title	**Average Earnings**	**Job Growth**	**Job Openings**
1. Administrative Services Managers	$62,300	16.9%	25,000
2. Business Teachers, Postsecondary	$58,230	32.2%	329,000
3. Chief Executives	$141,820	14.9%	38,000
4. Logisticians	$59,460	13.2%	7,000
5. Storage and Distribution Managers	$67,300	12.7%	15,000
6. Transportation Managers	$67,300	12.7%	15,000

Job 2 shares 329,000 job openings with 35 jobs not included in the list. Jobs 5 and 6 share 15,000 job openings.

Characteristics of the Related Jobs: Interests—Enterprising; Conventional; Social. Skills—Management of financial resources; management of personnel resources; coordination; systems evaluation; systems analysis. Values—Authority; autonomy; responsibility; creativity; working conditions. Work Conditions—Sitting; indoors, environmentally controlled; walking and running.

Urban Studies

Focuses on the application of social science principles to the study of urban institutions and the forces influencing urban social and political life. Related CIP Program: 45.1201 Urban Studies/Affairs.

Specializations in the Major: Community economic development, environmental design, ethnic studies, urban economics, urban planning, urban politics.

Typical Sequence of College Courses: English composition, introduction to economics, introduction to sociology, statistics for business and social sciences, urban politics, history of cities, urban economics, introduction to urban planning, public policy analysis, seminar (reporting on research). Typical Sequence of High School Courses: Algebra, English, foreign language, social science, trigonometry, history.

Career Snapshot: Many different kinds of activities are concentrated in cities and towns—economic, social, political, architectural, and cultural—so urban studies is an interdisciplinary major. Usually you can shape the major to concentrate on whichever of these aspects is of greatest interest to you. Degree holders go on to a variety of different careers, most often after getting a graduate or professional degree. Some work in urban planning or redevelopment, law, public administration, environmental planning, social work, or journalism.

Related Job			
Job Title	Average Earnings	Job Growth	Job Openings
Sociologists	$56,790	4.7%	fewer than 500

Characteristics of the Related Job: Interest—Investigative. Skills—Science; management of financial resources; writing; critical thinking; reading

© JIST Works

comprehension. **Values**—Creativity; autonomy; responsibility; working conditions; ability utilization. **Work Conditions**—Sitting; indoors, environmentally controlled.

Veterinary Medicine

Prepares individuals for the independent professional practice of veterinary medicine, involving the diagnosis, treatment, and health care management of animals and animal populations and the prevention and management of diseases that may be transmitted to humans. **Related CIP Program:** 51.2401 Veterinary Medicine (D.V.M.).

Specializations in the Major: Companion animals, large animals (horses, cattle), public health, research.

Typical Sequence of College Courses: English composition, introduction to psychology, college algebra, calculus, introduction to sociology, oral communication, general chemistry, general biology, introduction to computer science, organic chemistry, human anatomy and physiology, general microbiology, genetics, introduction to biochemistry, veterinary gross anatomy, neuroanatomy, veterinary histology and cell biology, veterinary radiology, animal nutrition and nutritional diseases, neuroanatomy, pathology, veterinary microbiology, pharmacology, veterinary ophthalmology, public health, veterinary surgery, reproduction, veterinary toxicology, clinical veterinary experience. **Typical Sequence of High School Courses:** English, algebra, geometry, trigonometry, biology, computer science, public speaking, chemistry, foreign language, physics, pre-calculus.

Career Snapshot: Veterinarians care for the health of animals—from dogs and cats to horses and cattle to exotic zoo animals—protect humans from diseases carried by animals, and conduct basic research on animal health. Most of them work in private practices. Some inspect animals or animal products for government agencies. Most students who enter the four-year veterinary school program have already completed a bachelor's degree that includes math and science coursework. Competition for entry to veterinary school is keen, but the job outlook is expected to be good.

Related Jobs			
Job Title	Average Earnings	Job Growth	Job Openings
1. Health Specialties Teachers, Postsecondary	$70,310	32.2%	329,000
2. Veterinarians	$68,280	17.4%	8,000

Job 1 shares 329,000 job openings with 35 jobs not included in the list.

Characteristics of the Related Jobs: Interests—Investigative; Social; Realistic. **Skills**—Science; instructing; reading comprehension; learning strategies; critical thinking. **Values**—Authority; creativity; social service; achievement; social status. **Work Conditions**—Exposed to disease or infections; exposed to radiation; indoors, environmentally controlled; specialized protective or safety equipment; contaminants.

Wildlife Management

Prepares individuals to conserve and manage wilderness areas and the flora and fauna therein, and manage wildlife reservations and zoological facilities for recreational, commercial, and ecological purposes. **Related CIP Program:** 03.0601 Wildlife and Wildlands Science and Management.

Specializations in the Major: Fisheries management, public policy, terrestrial wildlife management.

Typical Sequence of College Courses: English composition, calculus, general biology, general chemistry, organic chemistry, oral communication, statistics, introduction to computer science, introduction to soil science, ecology, general zoology, ecology, introduction to wildlife conservation, invertebrate zoology, introduction to forestry, mammalogy, ornithology, natural resource biometrics, wildlife habitat management, animal population dynamics and management, animal physiology, ichthyology/herpetology, regional wildlife management and policy. **Typical Sequence of High School Courses:** Biology, chemistry, algebra, geometry, trigonometry, computer science, English, public speaking, geography.

Career Snapshot: The study of wildlife management combines a number of disciplines, including biology and public policy. Wildlife managers have to understand how wild creatures interact with their natural environment and how they react to the pressures put on them by human hunting and habitat destruction. Most wildlife managers work for governmental agencies. Students who specialize in fisheries management may find work in the growing field of aquaculture.

Related Jobs			
Job Title	Average Earnings	Job Growth	Job Openings
1. Fish and Game Wardens	$42,310	10.5%	1,000
2. Park Naturalists	$52,330	6.3%	2,000
3. Range Managers	$52,330	6.3%	2,000
4. Soil Conservationists	$52,330	6.3%	2,000
5. Zoologists and Wildlife Biologists	$50,680	13.0%	1,000

Jobs 2, 3, and 4 share 2,000 job openings.

Characteristics of the Related Jobs: Interests—Investigative; Realistic. **Skills**—Science; persuasion; negotiation; management of financial resources; writing. **Values**—Autonomy; creativity; responsibility; ability utilization; achievement. **Work Conditions**—Outdoors, exposed to weather; very hot or cold; minor burns, cuts, bites, or stings; extremely bright or inadequate lighting; specialized protective or safety equipment.

Women's Studies

Focuses on the history, sociology, politics, culture, and economics of women, and the development of modern feminism in relation to the roles played by women in different periods and locations in North America and the world. **Related CIP Program:** 05.0207 Women's Studies.

Specializations in the Major: Feminist theory, history of feminism, women's issues in art and culture, women's political issues.

Typical Sequence of College Courses: English composition, foreign language, American history, introduction to women's studies, women of color, theories of feminism, historical and philosophical origins of feminism, feminism from a global perspective, seminar (reporting on research). **Typical Sequence of High School Courses:** English, algebra, foreign language, history, literature, public speaking, social science.

Career Snapshot: Women's studies is an interdisciplinary major that looks at the experience of women from the perspectives of history, literature, psychology, and sociology, among others. Graduates of this major may go into business fields where understanding of women's issues can be helpful—for example, advertising or human resources management. With further education, they may also find careers in fields where they can affect the lives of women, such as social work, law, public health, or public administration.

Related Job			
Job Title	Average Earnings	Job Growth	Job Openings
Area, Ethnic, and Cultural Studies Teachers, Postsecondary	$55,660	32.2%	329,000

This job shares 329,000 job openings with 35 jobs not included in the list.

Characteristics of the Related Job: Interests—Social; Investigative; Artistic. **Skills**—Writing; instructing; critical thinking; persuasion; active learning. **Values**—Authority; social service; creativity; achievement; social status. **Work Conditions**—Sitting; indoors, environmentally controlled.

Zoology

Focuses on the scientific study of the biology of animal species and phyla, with reference to their molecular and cellular systems, anatomy, physiology, and behavior. **Related CIP Program:** 26.0701 Zoology/Animal Biology.

Specializations in the Major: Entomology, herpetology, ichthyology, mammalogy, ornithology.

Typical Sequence of College Courses: English composition, calculus, introduction to computer science, general chemistry, general biology, organic chemistry, genetics, general physics, cell biology, statistics, animal anatomy and physiology, evolution, ecology. **Typical Sequence of High School Courses:** English, biology, algebra, geometry, trigonometry, chemistry, precalculus, physics, computer science, calculus.

Career Snapshot: Zoologists study any form of animal life and therefore need a good background in biology and chemistry. A bachelor's degree in zoology can be a good first step toward a professional degree in medicine, veterinary science, or dentistry, or it may lead to entry-level work in some

© JIST Works

government and business fields. A graduate degree in zoology is good preparation for a career in research, college teaching, or agricultural extension service.

Related Jobs			
Job Title	Average Earnings	Job Growth	Job Openings
1. Biological Science Teachers, Postsecondary	$63,750	32.2%	329,000
2. Natural Sciences Managers	$90,080	13.6%	5,000
3. Zoologists and Wildlife Biologists	$50,680	13.0%	1,000

Job 1 shares 329,000 job openings with 35 jobs not included in the list.

Characteristics of the Related Jobs: Interest—Investigative. **Skills**—Science; instructing; active learning; writing; reading comprehension. **Values**—Authority; creativity; autonomy; ability utilization; responsibility. **Work Conditions**—Hazardous conditions; indoors, environmentally controlled; exposed to disease or infections; contaminants; common protective or safety equipment.

Key Points: Chapter 6

- Several majors described in this chapter are worth your consideration because they're a good match for you and are linked to careers that are attractive to you.

- When you consider a major, consider the whole package: the high school program that precedes it, the courses and specialization you'll study, and the careers it leads to. Be sure you feel comfortable with all of them.

- If the information you find in this chapter has raised some additional questions in your mind—good! Don't make a commitment until you have investigated further. But at least you've gotten a great start.

Index

© JIST Works

© JIST Works

© JIST Works

© JIST Works

I

J–K

L

M

© JIST Works

© JIST Works

© JIST Works

© JIST Works

© *JIST Works*